MANSFIELD
Past in Pictures

MANSFIELD
Past in Pictures

The Old Mansfield Society
Founded in 1919

First published in Great Britain in 2008 by
The Breedon Books Publishing Company Limited

This paperback edition published in Great Britain in 2020
by DB Publishing, an imprint of JMD Media Ltd

ISBN 978-1-78091-425-1

Printed and bound in the UK

CONTENTS

INTRODUCTION

The Old Mansfield Society was established in 1919 and celebrated it's Centenary Year in 2019 with a highly successful exhibition of it's archived material in the Mansfield Museum. The success of the exhibition has rekindled much local interest in the history of the town prompting the reprint of this publication.

The Society was the idea of three eminent local citizens, Mr Albert Sorby Buxton a local artist of some repute, Mr John Harrop White a solicitor, town clerk and a pillar of the Old Meeting House (he was born in the town's Swan Hotel in 1856!) and Alderman Daniel H. Maltby, proprietor of a private school, a leading member of the United Reform Church and Mayor of the Borough in 1914.

There is little doubt that Mr Buxton was the driving force behind the establishment of the Society, he had been a student of the famous London Slade School of Art and was head of, and instrumental in the establishment of the Mansfield School of Art. His lasting legacy to the town can be seen in the Museum, where his collection of water colours, donated on his death in 1932, depict local scenes of 'Old Mansfield' and are on permanent display.

The aims of the Society are to preserve photographic images and facts about the town and to support the preservation of the heritage and important buildings of the locality.

The photographs that can be seen in this book have come from members of the public and newspapers. People and organisations like the Old Mansfield Society, have collected or produced these photographs to make them available to a much wider and appreciative public. The commentaries accompanying the images have come from those who have contributed, but in many cases the information may be amplified by the public who are invited to submit any relevant facts thus enabling them too to take an active part in preserving our heritage. This is very important as 'History' is not just about national or international events but also about the seemingly unimportant everyday lives of those that build up a gigantic 'Social History' of how and where people lived and worked, especially if, because of inevitable changes in our towns cities and villages, these memories are lost.

We all enjoy looking at old photographs and reminiscing, but how often do we realise that costume, buildings or location all add up to 'how we used to live', and so we should be proud to let our memories be seen and shared by future generations.

CEREMONIES AND ROYALTY

Fortunately for the crowds of people gathered outside the town hall the weather was kind – 'all that could be desired', it was reported – on Tuesday 14 July 1891. The official party, together with many officials and representatives of various organisations in the town, had proceeded from the railway station, and those assembled in the Market Place listened intently while the acting mayor, Mr G.H. Hibbert, and the acting town clerk, Mr R.J. Parsons, introduced and proclaimed the Charter of Incorporation of the Borough. There was a general sense of achievement and enthusiasm, and everything possible had been done to make the occasion memorable. Celebrations extended over three days, featuring the Mansfield Company of Rifle Volunteers, the Sherwood Rangers Yeomanry, several bands (including the Nottingham Sax-Tuba Band, Pleasley Colliery Band and the Workhouse Drum and Fife Band), feasting, a dinner for old people (over 60 years of age) and an extension of the licensing hours from 11pm to midnight (despite protests from the Women's Temperance Association). There were flags, floral arches, banners, bells, lights and fireworks everywhere. After the ceremony, at the town hall, a fête on the recreation ground attracted the crowd to see acrobats, conjurors, bands, a quadrille and other amusements. There was a general sense that Mansfield had come of age and could look to the future with confidence.

Residents from the Union Street area are shown here outside the Hope and Anchor, displaying, by their presence and street decorations, their support and enthusiasm for the Incorporation of the Borough celebrations in July 1891.

SRIY 'A' Squadron, Mansfield Camp, 1906

Had a similar photograph to this been taken a few years earlier, these men would have been resplendent in their dress uniforms of green and gold. Since then the army had learnt from campaigns in South Africa that, however splendid such a turnout might look on the parade ground, it had its disadvantages on the battlefield. Thus, in 1906, when these Mansfield men of 'A' Squadron of the Sherwood Rangers Yeomanry assembled for their annual camp, they wore the drab and less conspicuous khaki. The Sherwood Rangers were a territorial regiment; the men were part-timers ('Saturday Soldiers') who trained at weekends and at their annual camp.

Civic occasion in the Market Place

The size of the crowd in this photograph that had gathered in the Market Place suggests that this was an occasion of some importance, though it is not clear what it was. However, the presence of the mace bearer, mayor, town clerk and town councillors, suggests that it was significant. Lining the Market Place to the left are members of the local territorial units. Nearest the camera, eye-catching in their plumed busbies and green and gold, are members of the Sherwood Rangers Yeomanry, while next to them in peaked caps, scarlet and blue, are the foot soldiers of the Sherwood Foresters. Could the popular music hall song of the day boast that 'there's something about a soldier'?

The royal visit by King George V and Queen Mary on 25 June 1914 began at Welbeck Abbey and then pursued a route through Creswell, Clowne, Bolsover, Shirebrook and Pleasley to arrive at the town hall in Mansfield a little before noon. The royal visitors were greeted at the dais by the Duke of Portland and the Mayor of Mansfield (Ald. T. Taylor, JP). The chairman of the hospital management board (Mr H.E. Hollins) invited the king to formally open the new King Edward Memorial Wing, which he did with a gesture to modern technology by pressing a button connected electrically to the main entrance door of the hospital. The discharge of a rocket signified its opening, acknowledged by a small, controlled explosion at the town hall. Shortly afterwards the royal party left to visit the works at Barringer Wallis & Manners before continuing their tour via Forest Town, Newstead Abbey, Hucknall, Kimberley and returning to Welbeck.

The public reception for Corporal Fuller, VC, in front of the town hall on 2 June 1915. The crowds were estimated to be 20,000. Wilfred Dolby Fuller (born 28 July 1893 in East Kirby, near Mansfield) received the Victoria Cross when he was just 21 years old. Before the outbreak of World War One he had moved to Mansfield and worked as a pony driver at Mansfield colliery until he joined the Grenadier Guards in 1911. On 12 March 1915 at Neuve Chapelle, France, Lance-Corporal Fuller saw a party of the enemy trying to escape along a communication trench. He ran towards them and killed the leading man with a bomb; the remainder (nearly 50), seeing no way of evading his bombs, all surrendered to him. Fuller was quite alone at the time. He received his Victoria Cross from King George V at Buckingham Palace on 4 June 1915. In September of the same year, at the express wish of the Tsar of Russia, he was also decorated by the king with the Russian Order of St George. He married in 1916, and later the same year he was discharged from the army on medical grounds and joined the Somerset Constabulary. He retired from the police service on medical grounds in 1940 and took up residence in Frome, where he died in 1947.

The Prince of Wales, later to succeed his father, George V, as King Edward VIII in 1936 before abdicating in the same year, paid a visit to Mansfield on 1 August 1923. It does not appear to have been a visit with any specific purpose, and seems to have been slipped in between a social visit to the Duke of Portland's seat at Welbeck Abbey and an official engagement in Nottingham. He was then, and later, a popular member of the Royal family and given a hugely enthusiastic welcome in Mansfield, not least by the crowds of children for whose benefit the prince requested a school holiday. The prince is seen here on the steps of the town hall, where he was introduced by the duke and briefly addressed the crowd filling the Market Place. With him can be seen the mayor, Henry Daniel.

This event may possibly be the 1927 Market Charter Anniversary (although the style of clothing, particularly the Duchess's hat, appears to indicate a slightly earlier date). The first Duke of Portland attained Peerage of Great Britain in 1716. This was William Henry Bentinck, who was already Earl of Portland. The dukedom came into the possession of the Cavendish-Bentinck family by marriage and the family have quite an extensive history. The 3rd Duke of Portland, William Henry Cavendish Bentinck, 3rd Duke of Portland, Marquess of Titchfield, Earl of Portland, Viscount Woodstock, Baron of Cirencester (14 April 1738–30 October 1809) was the most famous, as statesman and Prime Minister. The 5th Duke was an eccentric recluse who shunned visitors. He had 15 miles of tunnels dug under the house, which housed libraries, a billiard room large enough for 12 full-size tables and an enormous subterranean ballroom large enough to take 2,000 dancers – all of which remained unused. When in London, the duke always travelled in a closed carriage, maintained a shuttered box at the opera and kept the curtains permanently drawn at the windows of his substantial town house in Cavendish Square. The duke seen here is the 6th Duke of Portland, William John Arthur Charles James Cavendish-Bentinck (1857–1943), who was duke between 1879–1943. The dukedom of Portland became extinct on the 9th Duke's death, though his distant cousin succeeded him as Earl of Portland.

The Duchess of Portland at an ox roast for the hospital carnival of 1932 on Chesterfield Road recreation ground. The chef, Mr Tyler of Stratford-upon-Avon, is speaking to the Duchess of Portland, wife of the 6th Duke of Portland, William John Arthur Charles James Cavendish-Bentinck (1857–1943), who was duke between 1879 and 1943. Her name was Winifred (Winifred Dallas-Yorke, died 30 July 1954).

Before she succeeded her father, King George VI, to the throne, Princess Elizabeth, accompanied by the Duke of Edinburgh, paid a visit to Mansfield on 29 June 1949. They are shown here in the company of the mayor, Ald. J.G. Pratt, before the princess formally laid the foundation stone for the Portland Training College for the Disabled.

Queen Elizabeth, consort of King George VI, is pictured here on 24 July 1950 when she visited Mansfield to officially celebrate the opening of Portland Training College, ceremonially founded by her daughter, the then Princess Elizabeth, the previous year.

Arrival at the library

One of the events commemorating the ascention of Queen Elizabeth II was a visit to Mansfield on 28 July 1977, when she was greeted by the Lord Lieutenant of the County, Commander Philip Franklin. It was on the occasion of this Silver Jubilee visit that the new library was officially declared open by the Queen.

Signing the visitors' book in the town hall.

The crowds before.

…and after the visit.

John Ogdon was born on 27 January 1937 at Mansfield Woodhouse. However it was in Mansfield where he took his first lesson in playing the piano. His teacher was Miss Nellie Houseley, and it was she who first recognised his outstanding talent and laid the foundation of discipline and technique so necessary for its full development. After studying at the Royal College of Music in Manchester his career began dramatically when he took the place of an indisposed artist and the sheer brilliance of his playing astounded the audience. The climax of his skill and virtuosity came in 1962 when he was declared a joint winner of the prestigious Tchaikovsky competition in Moscow. Thereafter, illness tended to limit his career, though it did nothing to diminish his genius. Sadly, he died on 1 August 1989. John Ogdon always retained a warm affection for Mansfield, visiting the town regularly and delighting local audiences with his playing. Perhaps the most memorable of these occasions was in 1983 when he accompanied the Mansfield Choral Society in a performance of Franz Liszt's oratorio Christus. This photograph was taken shortly afterwards and shows him sitting beside Pamela Cook, founder and conductor of the widely acclaimed Cantamus Choir, and, behind him, David Chamberlain, conductor of the Choral Society, alongside the four soloists.

The official opening of the Territorial Army Centre on Bath Street, on the 30 March 1985, was performed by Mr Dennis Thatcher, a former major in the TA and husband of Mrs Margaret (now Lady) Thatcher, then Prime Minister. The centre, built at a cost of £1.4 million, is impressive, with a central drill hall, adjoining lecture rooms and administrative offices, a sub-basement providing car parking and a .22 rifle range, a garage and workshop complex and accommodation for a caretaker. The 'landlord' unit is 'A' company of the 3rd (Volunteer) Battn., Worcs. and Sherwood Foresters Regiment (now part of the Mercian Regiment), whose then Commanding Officer, Lt. Col. N. Cullen, accepted the keys from the President of East Midlands TAVRA, Col. R.A. Martin.

One of the memorable features of the Princess Royal's visit to Mansfield on 29 November 1991 was her arrival by helicopter at the Civic Centre to be met by the Lord Lieutenant, Sir Andrew Buchanan. Her first mission was to unveil a plaque at the Rock Valley Development, a scheme conceived and financed by Mansfield District Council, East Midlands Housing Association, Nottinghamshire County Council and the European Development Fund, offering 57 affordable flats to childless and single occupiers. She went on to plant a 'semi-mature' oak-tree to mark the opening of Riverside Walkway and caused some admiration and hilarity by her approach to the task, described in reports of the event as 'robust'. After a stroll along the Walkway, she was taken by car to perform the official opening of the Water Meadows, a leisure and pool complex, complete with wave machine and 30-metre flume, built at a cost of £6.25 million.

CHURCHES

St John's Church

During the 19th century the population of Mansfield increased fourfold, and new houses to accommodate the greater number of people stretched out into what had hitherto been open countryside. To keep pace with the needs of this growth, both Anglicans and non-conformists built new places of worship, some of them in the expanding parts of the town. Early off the mark were the Anglicans with St John's Church, seen in this picture. It was completed and dedicated for worship by the Bishop of Lincoln, the Rt Revd John Jackson (1811–1885), on 29 July 1856 and provided seating for a congregation of 1,000 people. Mainly of Mansfield stone, it remains a striking feature of the townscape.

St. Mark's Church, Mansfield.

High altar

St Mark's Church

Not as imposing as St John's, the foundation stone of St Mark's Church was laid by the Duke of Portland on 26 May 1896. Its design was the work of the London-based architect, Temple Moore. The vicar Revd Arthur Henley, was drowned while on holiday during its construction. When a parish hall was added in 1909 it was named the Henley Memorial Hall in his memory. In this photograph the church has a 'new' look to it and was probably taken shortly after its completion.

The Friends' Meeting House

By the end of the 19th century, non-conformist chapels and meeting houses of several denominations were regular features of Mansfield's streets. Although their meeting house was not built until the 1790s, the Society of Friends, or Quakers, had already been in existence in the town for over 100 years. In fact, their records go back to 1671. This photograph shows their burial ground and meeting house and was taken just before the demolition of the latter in 1974 to make way for the inner ring road and car parking spaces. Its one-time existence is marked by Quaker Way on the present-day town plan.

The Methodist New Connexion Chapel, St John's Street

Little is known of the activities of the Methodist New Connexion chapel. After taking over the Wesleyans' chapel on Stockwell Gate, they stayed there until 1810 when they sold the building. Perhaps it was too large for their needs or too expensive to maintain because they were never strongly supported. However, by 1839 they felt sufficiently confident to build the chapel shown in this photograph. Sadly, its service in that capacity was short: by 1870 it had been closed and sold to a firm of hosiery manufacturers who used it as a warehouse. Today, with its external appearance altered little, it is a furniture store.

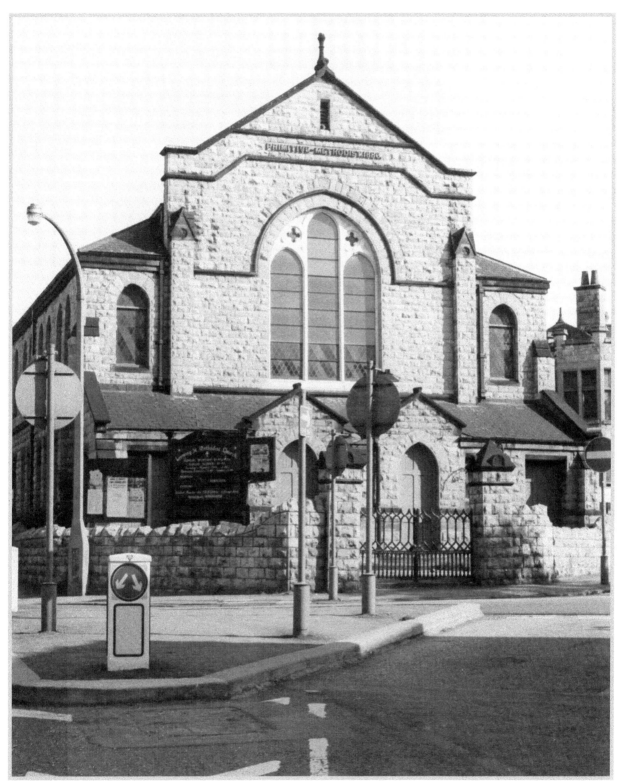

The Primitive Methodist Chapel, Leeming Street
The Primitive Methodists established a society in Mansfield in 1818. Mainly supported by those who worked in factories, mills, mines and on the farms, they initially favoured street and 'camp' meetings, but as the 19th century progressed they became more chapel-centred. In Mansfield they began with a converted cottage, then moved to a purpose-built place of worship on Queen Street (it still stands) until the chapel shown in this picture was completed, in 1887. Methodist union in 1932 and the general decline in church attendance made it redundant and it was closed in 1960. After some years of disuse it was, in 1986, taken over by the Church of the God of Prophecy who still worship in it today.

St Lawrence's Church and the dedication of the Church Hall
St Lawrence's Church was built in 1909 on the junction of Skerry Hill and Pecks Hill, replacing a mission room which had been a place for worship and associated activities since 1887. It was one attempt, among several, to provide for the needs of an ever-increasing population that took place in the second half of the 19th century.

A hundred years later the mission room, long used as a church hall, was inadequate in size and amenity and had been badly damaged by fire. It was replaced, and in 1992 the new building was dedicated with appropriate ecclesiastical ceremony by the Rt Revd Patrick Harris, the Bishop of Southwell. This photograph shows the bishop with the parochial clergy, the Revds J. Burgess and W. Porter and the churchwardens, Messrs R. Troop and D. Colley.

The Congregational Chapel, Westgate

During the second half of the 19th century many non-conformist societies, whose chapels were tucked away out of sight down back streets, aspired to greater prominence. So it was with the Congregationalists at Mansfield. In 1878 they moved from Quaker Lane into their almost-complete new place of worship at the top of Westgate at its junction with Westfield Lane. Designed by the Mansfield-born, though Nottingham-based, architect Watson Fothergill, it stood out from all its neighbouring buildings and completely overshadowed the odd little cast-iron gents' urinal situated just in front of it. The chapel was used until 1981 and demolished soon afterwards, to be replaced by a doctor's surgery.

The Wesleyan/Baptist Chapel, Stockwell Gate

A flattering camera angle makes this look a more imposing building than it actually was. It was built for the Wesleyan Methodists in 1791, but their use of it was brief. A breakaway faction, subsequently known as the Methodist New Connexion, seized the chapel and used it until they moved to new premises on St John's Street. After a period of varied occupancy it was acquired by the Baptists, who remained there until 1912, when their new chapel was opened nearby on Rosemary Street. Even then, they continued to use this building as a Sunday school.

The Baptist Chapel, Rosemary Street
Below is a photograph of the Baptist chapel that replaced that on the preceding picture. Framed between the Empire cinema and the Belle Vue Inn (both since demolished), it was taken around 1970, prior to its demolition two years later. Externally it resembled an Anglican church rather than a non-conformist chapel, this being the trend at the time. The United Methodist church on Nottingham Road is another example in the town. As it succumbed to the bulldozer, the Baptists moved further up Rosemary Street to their present place of worship.

St Peter's Church

For around 900 years St Peter's Church has been the principal place of worship and the focal point for much that has happened in the town. Indeed, it may stand on the site of an earlier building as Mansfield was a Saxon settlement and a church is mentioned in the Domesday Book of 1086. This photograph was taken in around 1900 at 2.30pm on a wintry afternoon from the bottom of Church Street. Over the years the church has been altered, enlarged, repaired and restored so that it now bears little resemblance to its first appearance. One of the oldest surviving parts is clearly shown in this picture. It is the lower section of the tower with its thick, solid-looking stonework, tiny windows and round-arched doorway: all typical of the Norman-style of building.

This photograph was taken from Toothill Lane, some years after the previous picture. The more modern streetlight gives a clue to its later date, though the surrounding buildings date back to the 18th century. Even the distant gasometer, perhaps looking a little out of place, had been there for about 100 years.

J. Seddon Tyrer, a respected Mansfield artist of the second-half of the 19th century, painted this picture of the interior of St Peter's Church just before it was transformed by restoration work carried out in 1870 and 1871. The old pews were replaced, the side galleries removed, a new organ installed and much clutter that had accumulated over the years was taken out. Even with the cramped seating shown in the picture, it is difficult to see where the 1,500 adults who, the vicar claimed, were at the evening service on the 30 March 1851 could have sat.

The Old Meeting House, Stockwell Gate

The Old Meeting House was appropriately named as it is the longest surviving non-conformist place of worship in the town. It was built in 1702 and radically restored in 1870–71, while the prominent porch was added in 1940 in memory of Mrs Agnes Mary Harrop White, wife of a prominent church member and influential townsman. The church was founded after five dissenting Anglican clergymen were ejected from their Nottingham livings under the Act of Uniformity of 1662. They subsequently settled in Mansfield and a congregation grew up around them. Originally regarded as Presbyterians, they were later known as Unitarians, a designation they still hold. This photograph was taken in around 1970.

The Old Meeting House Parsonage, Stockwell Gate

Seen from Stockwell Gate, as on this photograph of 1970, the parsonage of the Old Meeting House presents a picture of 18th-century symmetry among the hotch-potch of later buildings that now cluster around it. It was built a few years before the Old Meeting House and bequeathed to the church in 1706. To the right of the gateway is a stone memorial tablet engraved with the names of members who were killed in war. Although healthier financially than many non-conformist churches, the Sale of Work poster indicates that the Old Meeting House had to arrange fund-raising events to help pay its way.

Independent Meeting House, Quaker Lane
In 1790 another non-conformist group began holding services in the town. They were the Independents, later known as Congregationalists. By 1793 they felt strong enough to build their own meeting house, which was down Quaker Lane, almost facing that of the Society of Friends, after whom the lane was named. Later, in 1878, they moved to their new Congregational Chapel on Westgate, and the old building was taken over by George Pickard for his jam factory a few years later. This photograph, taken in 1948, shows the gateway leading into the chapel grounds. The building to the right of the picture, partly in view, was the chapel; the long extension standing to the left was the school room which was added in 1829. The site was cleared in 1974 due to the demands of the inner ring road.

EDUCATION

Thompson's Charity School, Toothill Lane

After surviving the Lisbon earthquake of 1755, Charles Thompson (1714–1784) returned to Mansfield and spent the rest of his life helping the poorer people of his native town. In his will, he left £600 to help the charity which had been set up after the death of Samuel Brunts in 1711. Brunts had wanted the money to be used to help assist the poor in the apprenticing and educating of their children. Until 1787 his charity had sent apprentices out to various masters and mistresses in the town. Thompson's bequest was also to be used for the better education of the poor children of the town and, to this end, land was bought for the Brunts' Trustees to build a school. The architect was McLellan, who worked on other projects in the town. Work began in 1786 and was finished by 12 June 1787. By 1790, 30 boys from Thompson's Charity and 30 girls and 10 boys from Brunts' Charity were being educated there. The school closed in 1891, when it was absorbed into the new Brunts' Technical School on Woodhouse Road.

The Old Grammar School in St Peter's Churchyard was granted its charter by Queen Elizabeth I in 1561 and the original premises had places for 36 boys. By the early 18th century the old school had become obsolete and, in 1714, Queen Anne, as Lady of the Manor of Mansfield, provided 20 loads of timber from Sherwood Forest to help with the rebuilding. Further restoration took place in 1851, during the reign of Queen Victoria.

In 1878, with the opening of Queen Elizabeth's Grammar School for Boys on Chesterfield Road, the churchyard building became a mixed infant and junior national school, and later a Church of England national school.

In 1974 pupils were transferred to the new St Peter's School on the Bellamy Road estate and the old premises came to be used as a Parish Centre. In 1997 the building was fully restored and refurbished with funding from the National Lottery Charities Board.

Faith Clerkson Charity School

In her will, dated 1725, Mrs Faith Clerkson bequeathed £2,000 to be used for beneficial purposes and, in 1737, a school was built on what later became the corner of Station Street and Albert Street. Thirty boys and 30 girls received free tuition, while others paid a small fee. By 1820 there were 80 pupils – 40 boys who were taught reading, writing and arithmetic and 40 girls who learned reading, writing, accounts, sewing and knitting. Every Sunday the scholars attended the parish church. The boys wore woollen caps, blue cut-away coats with red buttons, knee breeches and buckled shoes, and the girls felt bonnets, blue baize, or serge, frocks and white aprons. The building, which dates from 1849, was taken over by Maltby's Academy when the Faith Clerkson School closed in 1887. It ceased to be a school in 1900 and was demolished in 1974. The site is now the approach to the Robin Hood Line railway station and St Peter's retail park.

William Espin's Commercial Academy

Mr Espin came to Mansfield in the early 19th century and opened a private school. This venture proved so successful that he later moved to larger premises (Grove House) and began to take in boarders. This engraved announcement, which he designed himself, shows the spire of St Peter's Church in the background and defines the location of his academy. The surveying and mathematical instruments, the classical building and the globe signify the range of education available. The beehive demonstrates the industry to be found there. The main purpose of the engraving was to announce the reopening of his 'English, Mathematical and Commercial Academy' on 25 January 1819, and it sets out his terms. Boarders were to pay 20 guineas per annum, plus one gn entrance fee and one gn in lieu of sheets. If they required tea for breakfast it would cost them two gns pa (tea was an expensive luxury in 1819). All scholars had to provide their own pens, ink and books.

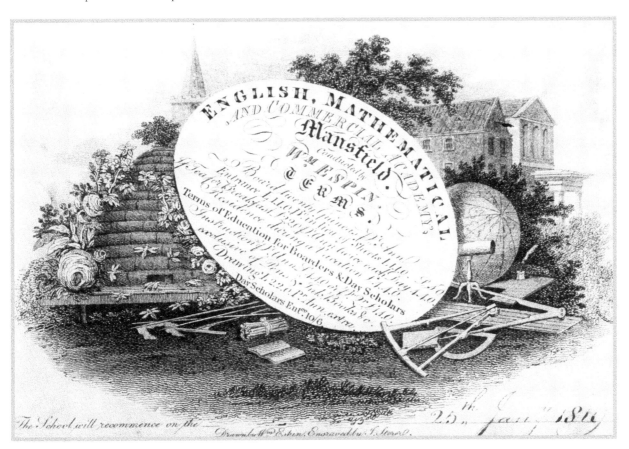

Maltby's Academy

John Maltby opened his private academy in 1836 catering mainly for the sons of local shopkeepers and professional men. Over the years, three generations of the Maltby family ran the academy in a three-storey building in Rock Court, off Bridge Street. Daniel H. Maltby assisted his father and succeeded him as headmaster in 1886. After 51 years in Rock Valley, the Academy moved to the former premises of the Faith Clerkson Charity School on Albert Street, where it remained until July 1928, having completed 92 years of existence. The original Rock Court building has now been restored and divided into flats.

Rock Court

John Maltby

Miss Susannah Parsons – Carte de Visite, dated 1862
Miss Parsons and her sister Jane ran a school at Westgate House from the 1830s until 1877. Children from Mansfield's leading families were educated there and subjected to strict discipline. Two former pupils were William Jackson Chadburn (mayor in 1899) and Douglas J. Patterson (mayor in 1892), who scratched his initials on the old pantry window.

Brunts' School, Woodhouse Road

In 1891 permission was given to close Thompson's Charity School on Toothill Lane and to build Brunts' Technical School on Woodhouse Road. The foundation stone was laid in 1893 and the school was officially opened by Lord Belper in 1894, with places for 200 pupils. The curriculum was varied and aimed to give an education between elementary and grammar school levels. However, there was a leaning towards practical subjects with provision for sciences, domestic studies and workshops. After the 1944 Education Act, Brunts' became a secondary grammar school and continued taking pupils from Mansfield and the surrounding districts. After 1974, when the 11+ selection examinations were dropped, it became a Comprehensive School, its pupils coming from the local catchment area. With the closure of the middle schools, a new site on Windmill Lane was built to accommodate the extra intake. Today, over a century later, it is now Brunts' Community Comprehensive School, catering for an age range of 11 to 18 years.

BRUNTS SCHOOL, MANSFIELD   G 9847

St John's School, St John's Street

During the mid-19th century, when St Peter's became too small to serve the growing population, it was decided to build a new church and school on Catlow Street, which became St John's Street. The school, for both infants and juniors, opened in 1862. The children attended a weekly service in the church and underwent a yearly inspection in Religious Education. Later St John's became a senior school and then, after the 1944 Education Act which divided senior education into three categories, it became a secondary modern school with pupils aged 11 to 15. In 1974 it became a middle school, transferring its 14+ pupils to Brunts' Upper School. When middle schools were closed, all pupils aged 11+ were transferred to upper schools. The original school is currently serving a new purpose as a parish centre.

Queen Elizabeth's Grammar School for Boys

The separation between St Peter's Church and the Old Grammar School led to the building of the Queen Elizabeth's Grammar School for Boys on Chesterfield Road. It was opened in 1874 and dedicated to continuing the same high Christian standards of the former school, with an emphasis on the virtues of hard work and aiming for high academic levels and standards of conduct and dress. The old, rather narrow curriculum was broadened to include science and commercial subjects. Sporting activities were now considered to be an important part of a boy's education. The maximum school fee was £12 per annum, but there were some scholarship places available. Originally, boarding facilities were offered and there was also a preparatory department which admitted boys at eight years of age. After the 1944 Education Act, it became a secondary grammar and later a comprehensive school. In 1993 it merged with the Queen Elizabeth's Girls' Comprehensive, and in 1997 was visited by Queen Elizabeth II, who opened a new science block.

North-east corner of the quadrangle

Departure of Queen Elizabeth II, March 1997.

Queen Elizabeth's Grammar School for Girls, Woodhouse Road

The school was planned in 1875 and was temporarily based in two houses on Woodhouse Road. The new building was ready in 1891. It catered for an average of 170 pupils, which included the kindergarten for boys and girls up to eight years of age. The fees for the senior school were £2 13s 4d per term, but there were also some scholarship places. A high academic standard was expected and, as with the boys' grammar school, pupils were entered for the London Matriculation, Cambridge Local and Department of Science and Art Examinations. Good conduct and a neat appearance were considered essential, as were sporting activities, which included hockey, lacrosse and tennis. From the 1940s onwards it became, in turn, a secondary grammar, an upper and finally a comprehensive school. After the two Queen Elizabeth Schools were merged in 1993, the Woodhouse Road premises were redeveloped into private residential accommodation.

St Lawrence's School, Sandy Lane (c.1887)

This building dates from 1887 when it was used as a mission room until St Lawrence's Church was built in 1909. It was also used as a schoolroom, educating children aged five to 10 for a weekly fee of around 4d. By 1906 the surrounding area had become more developed and housed a greater number of people. By then these premises were too small to cope with the increasing school population, which was eventually transferred to the newly built Newgate Lane School. It was demolished in 1992, and St Lawrence's Community Centre now stands on this site. Several other similar schoolrooms, attached to churches and chapels, also flourished in the late-19th and early-20th centuries. These included St Mark's, Quarry Lane; the Wesleyan Mixed Infants, Stanhope Street; the Congregational British School, Wood Street; the Old Meeting House; and the Baptist Church Schools on Stockwell Gate. These all closed as the pupils were gradually absorbed into the new elementary schools.

Rosemary Street Schools

The Parliamentary Act of 1870 was designed to make elementary education available to all children. Gradually, with the passing of other acts, basic levels of education became free and compulsory, with the school leaving age rising from 11 in 1893 to 14 in 1918. Rosemary Street Elementary School, the first of several built between 1900 and 1919, was opened by Lord Belper two years after the election of Mansfield's School Board. This body took control of elementary education until 1903, when it was replaced by the Borough Education Committee. The building was designed by the Borough Architect R. Frank Vallance and catered for mixed infants and older boys and girls, who had their separate entrances, classrooms and play areas. The girls had a cookery centre, and among other up-to-date features were flushing outdoor toilets and hand-basins without taps or plugs. The caretaker had control of the water supply. In 1945 education became the responsibility of the West Notts Divisional Executive, and Rosemary Schools became a secondary modern, taking pupils from 11 to 15 years of age. In 1977 the pupils were transferred to modern purpose-built Secondary Schools and Rosemary School became the Science, Technology and General Studies (STAGS) Centre, an annexe of West Notts College. The building was demolished in 2002 and a block of privately owned apartments was built on the site.

Broomhill School, Broomhill Lane

Broomhill (1904) was one of the eight new elementary schools built in the early 19th century. Others were Pleasley Hill (1902), King Edward's (1903), Newgate Lane (1905), Carter Lane (1912), Moor Lane (1912) and Rainworth (1919).

Newgate Lane School
Newgate Lane School was built to serve an area which was expanding so rapidly that classes of over 40 were not uncommon. The children appear to be well-dressed but are all wearing sturdy hob-nailed boots. One of the boys in the centre of the front row of this class portrait, taken c.1900, is believed to be Herbert Baggaley.

Moor Lane School, c.1915

All Saints' Upper School (under construction), Rosemary Street
St Philip Neri's Roman Catholic Voluntary School opened on Ratcliffe Gate in 1877. In 1927 the school moved to Westfield Lane, which continued to be used as an infant and primary school after the opening of St Bede's Secondary School on Rosemary Street. This catered for children of Catholic families over a wide area. When completed, All Saints' Upper School took students aged 14+ and later became a comprehensive school with an age range of 11 to 16+. The infant and junior section, as St Philip Neri Primary School, moved into the Rosemary Street premises.

Technical College
In 1922 Ashfield House on Chesterfield Road, was purchased and used as a temporary technical school. Six years later, the students were moved to purpose-built premises fronting the main road, and in 1930 the School of Art moved from Carr Bank to Ashfield House, with A.S. Buxton as headmaster. In the 1950s, due to the urgent need for technical education, West Notts College of Further Education was built on Derby Road. The old premises were then used as a County Folk College, later joining with Ashfield House, which became the College of Arts. West Notts College is now one of the largest in the East Midlands, with Derby Road as its main campus and the Chesterfield Road premises as an important annexe.

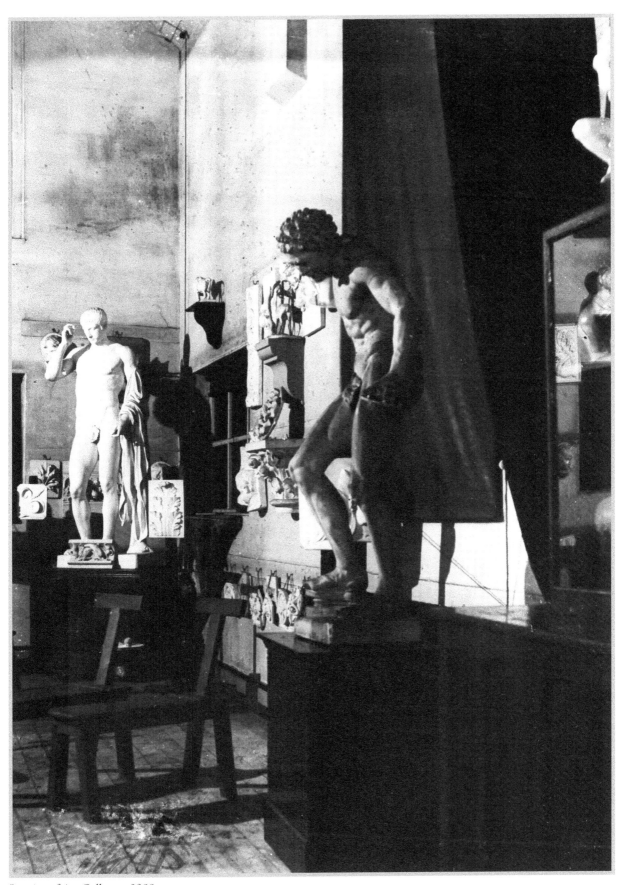

Interior of Art College, c.1900

Grove House, Brunts Street

Built as a manor house in the early 18th century, it was enlarged during the 19th century and opened as a private school by William Espin, who also taught for a time as usher and later headmaster at the grammar school until his death in 1865. Grove House continued to house a private school after the death of William Espin, run by Richard and William Tyrer and giving a classical and commercial education to the sons of prominent local residents (including the future town clerk John Harrop White). Their younger brother, Joseph Seddon Tyrer, was the Art Master, and he made several watercolour paintings of the area. They offered the teaching of 'the classics, mathematics, and the usual English subjects', included in the fees, which ranged from 12–16 guineas per annum for day scholars, to 30–35 guineas per annum for boarders. Extras could be taught at a fee of 1 guinea a quarter in French, German, drawing and land surveying. Also pupils would have to pay for music and dancing lessons, and the laundress charged 10–13 shillings per quarter for laundry. Later Grove House became the town house of William Jackson Chadburn, one of the partners in Mansfield Brewery. In 1919, after the Chadburn family moved out, the Duke of Portland gave the property to St Peter's Church. For almost 60 years parishioners used it as a Parochial Hall. By 1977 the building had fallen into such a state of disrepair that even though it was officially Grade II listed permission was given to demolish it.

Bottom of Blind Lane

This cottage once housed the assistant usher at the old grammar school, which was in the building behind the cottage. It was demolished c.1878 to widen the narrow corner onto Church Side. Blind Lane, which was opposite, was renamed in 1913 when the area around it, mainly the estate of Gilcroft, was redeveloped. It was given the name Midworth Street in memory of Samuel Midworth, a well-known 19th-century iron founder who had once owned Gilcroft House.

Redcliffe House, Ratcliffe Gate

From 1925 Redcliffe House was used a school clinic. Dental and medical services were available to all council schoolchildren, with treatment for minor ailments and conditions, such as ringworm. Eye-testing was also given, with free spectacles being provided if necessary. It is currently serving as a nursing home, run by Redcliffe House Limited.

Mansfield Womens' Suffragette Society had 70 members when this photograph was taken on Church Street in 1910. Monthly meetings were held at Miss Eileen Barringer's house on Crow Hill Drive. The branch was non-militant and non-party. The president was Miss Wright, the secretary was Mrs Manners and the treasurer was Mrs Barringer. The two latter ladies had a family connection with the tin box manufactory of Barringer, Wallis and Manners. The procession is passing the premises of the Public Benefit Boot Company, which sold cheap footwear.

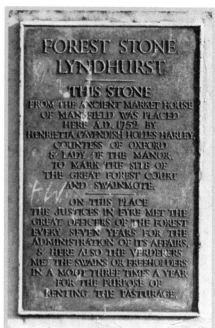

Forest Stone inscription

The Forest Stone at Lyndhurst was erected in the 18th century to mark the area where, tradition has it, the verderers, freeholders and Justices in Eyre met to adjudicate on matters concerning Sherwood and rentage of grazing, grievances and infringements of Forest Law. The old stone was traditionally said to have come from the first early Market House in Mansfield, pulled down in 1754 to be replaced with the Moot Hall. The Old Mansfield Society helped to renovate the site and also revived the Swainmote Feast, which took place at the Swan Inn on Church Street after the meeting at Lyndhurst. In 1922 the first dinner was held, attracting a large number of people to the Swan Hotel's dining room. Apart from the war years, the feast was held yearly until 1972, when lack of enthusiasm led to its cessation. The photograph below was taken in 1963, showing the Boar's head being carried in, accompanied by girls from High Oakham School singing the Boar's Head Carol.

Charles Thompson (1714–84) was a cloth merchant whose first business venture took him to Persia during the reign of Nadir Shah, who treated him honourably. When the Shah was assassinated in 1747, however, Thompson had to leave the country for England via Russia. His next, and last, business venture took him to Lisbon, Portugal, in 1750, where he prospered until the horrific earthquake of 1755 that killed over 60,000 people. While he survived the earthquake, his house was ruined and his money buried within it. Assuming all was lost, he returned to England, but his business partner persuaded him to return to Portugal and they were able to salvage their money from the cellar of the ruined house. Thompson took his share, returned to England and thence retired to his native Mansfield. He used to take regular walks from his house on Leeming Street to the spot where he chose to be buried, which at that time was well outside the town. His experiences in Lisbon of the earthquake throwing up bodies from their graves evidently affected him deeply, and he was determined to avoid the possibility of a similar occurrence. To prevent this, he gave instructions in his will that he be buried six yards deep, in the forest at the junction of the Southwell Turnpike road and Bury Lane (Berry Hill Lane). His wish that his funeral be very private was not heeded, as around 1,000 people followed his coffin from his house in Leeming Street to his final destination. In 1932 the Bishop of Southwell consecrated the grave and Brunts' Charity placed a plaque on the monument marking the site.

The 1907 photograph below illustrates one of the charities that Charles Thompson established in his will, whereby four-penny loaves were distributed to the poor on the steps of St Peter's Church on Good Friday.

Charles Thompson lived in a house on Leeming Street, later occupied by the chimney sweep Charles Wheat. The site later became premises for the Wakefield Building Society.

INNS

The Cattle Market Tavern, Nottingham Road

Until 1878 the site for cattle sales in Mansfield was Westgate and, for a year or two, the Market Place. The state of the streets on Mondays was deplorable, the filth defying description, and public pressure aided the construction of a purpose-built site on Nottingham Road. Mansfield-born architect Watson Fothergill designed the Market Tavern, and although the market site is now occupied by a large wet-leisure centre the tavern still stands, having undergone refurbishment and reopening as a restaurant called Lambs at the Market.

The Swan Hotel, Church Street
In 1508 the inn at the sign of the White Swan was part of a family property in a will. In the 18th century it became an important coaching inn with a coffee room, offering maps, magazines and newspapers for guests. Important visitors to the town stayed here, including Prince Leopold, youngest son of Queen Victoria, and in 1864 Mr and Mrs Charles Stratton, better known as General and Mrs Tom Thumb. In 1910 electricity was installed, and the old yard entrance was glazed over and became the main hotel entrance.

Nag's Head, Westgate

The Nag's Head dated back to the early 18th century. It was rebuilt and enlarged in 1875, but it closed and was demolished in 1979. The frontage, however, including the horse heads, was recreated in a new shop development.

The Nag's Head Yard was one of 10 narrow yards connecting West Gate to Back Lane West (Clumber Street), lined with stone-built properties dating from the 17th and 18th centuries. While the cottages appear to have stone paving on their frontages, the surface of the yard is rutted and uneven, no doubt muddy and treacherous in inclement weather. The water supply for household use could have been via a recently installed water mains at this time, but many old inhabitants of the town eschewed these 'new fangled' faucets and maintained that the so-called pure water had no flavour like the old well water, polluted as that was with enteric fever properties.

The White Hart, Westgate

This drawing above of the mediaeval White Hart Inn was made in the late 19th century by A.S. Buxton. In 1515 the inn was known as The Harte and owned by the Flogan Family. Bequeathed by Dame Cicely Flogan to endow a Chantry Priest in the then Catholic Church of St Peter, the property and the large estate of this family passed to the Trustees of Queen Elizabeth's Grammar School. Below, the back of the ancient White Hart Inn, with the entrance to White Hart Yard, was photographed in 1869, shortly before all the inhabitants shown were moved as their properties, as well as part of the inn, were pulled down to make way for the new railway viaduct. The White Hart was rebuilt in 1875 and can be seen next to the viaduct on the same photograph as the Swan Hotel.

The Old Blue Boar, Stockwell Gate

This inn was first mentioned in 1732 but may have been established well before then. The building, roofed with stone slabs, was one of many similar structures in the town, possibly timber-framed with cladding. In 1865 George Mallatratt became landlord. A successful businessman, occasional poacher, Unitarian and sportsman, he died in 1888 aged 56. His widow Mary left £100 in her will to found a bun distribution to children on Good Friday, a custom that still continues. The inn was rebuilt in 1888, closed in 1988 and is now a Building Society.

The Victoria Hotel, Albert Street
The Victoria Hotel on Albert Street was once known as the Cock Inn and at times as the Top White Bear. Albert Street was known, before Queen Victoria's marriage to Prince Albert, as the Cock Pit, appropriately as a pit existed at the rear of the old inn. Cock fighting was banned in 1844, although it illicitly continued undetected for many years after. Mansfield Brewery Company bought the old inn in 1878 for £2,140 and rebuilt it in 1922.

The Waggon & Coals Inn

In the 18th and early-19th centuries the town's main coal depot was situated at the Waggon & Coals Inn on Bridge Street. Mansfield's first gas works was built nearby in 1824. The inn had a large coal yard, six stables, a maltkiln and garden at the time of its sale in 1781. The landlord in the 1860s, Samuel Wilson, was a native of Farnsfield and had been a huntsman with the Rufford fox hounds. His brother was John Wilson of Grieves Lane, who hauled coal back to that village with a team of donkeys – up to 13 in number, led by one named Lion – which were needed to take a heavy load up the steep climb on Rock Hill. The inn was sold to Mansfield Brewery in 1887 for £1,680, and it fell victim to road improvements shortly after 1970.

John Wilson

King's Head, Stockwell Gate
The King's Head Inn was listed in a 1793 directory and in the early 19th century served as a stagecoach terminus for a service to Matlock. It was bought by Mansfield Brewery in 1888 for £1,600. It too was demolished during the Four Seasons development, but a new King's Head was opened on the site in 1975, only to be closed in 1995.

The Prince of Wales, Clerkson Street

The 19 March 1863 was the day that the future King Edward VII married Princess Alexandra of Denmark. As a celebration of this marriage, the proprietor of this beerhouse, George Else, the central figure in the group, had a photograph taken. The pub closed shortly afterwards, the premises becoming a laundry and later a plumbers. It was pulled down during the Inner Ring Road construction. To the left are the Elizabeth Heath's Almshouses on Nottingham Road.

Angel Inn, Westgate

Angel Yard, off Westgate, 1972. Named after the Angel Inn which formerly occupied the site, it vanished soon after this photograph was taken in the redevelopment which resulted in the Four Seasons shopping centre.

White Lion Inn, Church Street

Photographed in 1884, shortly before they were pulled down, this row of ancient properties on Church Street backed up to the Toothill Cliff. The White Lion pub was first recorded in 1732 but was probably opened well before then. Part of the premises had been hollowed out from the rock and shared steps led up to gardens on Toothill. One building in the yard was dated to 1584. During restoration in the 1990s, mud and reed ceilings, 16th-century fireplaces and painted wall decorations were found.

Ram Inn, Church Street
The Ram Inn on Church Street, known in the 18th century as the Shoulder of Mutton, is a late mediaeval building, where original timbers can be seen in the passage beside the inn, once known as Malt Kiln Court. In the 1850s the landlord Charles Ashmore doubled his income by working as sexton at the parish church. He bought a set of handbells which were rung after Sunday services. Mansfield Brewery Co. purchased the inn in 1897 for £1,800 from the Grammar School Trustees.

MILLS

The River Maun is now a tamed, safe river – almost a stream – but in former times, while never navigable, it was considerably stronger, wilder and more free, thus providing water and power for the textile industry. From the 13th century, textiles, in the form of sheeps' wool, was an industry in Mansfield, later to change to cotton, hosiery and knitwear. In the late 18th century seven mills were built along the Maun, providing a lucrative industry for a while.

Stanton Mill

In 1803 Charles Stanton bought, from the Duke of Newcastle, the site on Bath Lane and built his mill powered by water. He also built Carr Bank House on rising ground above the mill – perhaps so a discreet eye could be kept on the workers' activities. Later, both mill and house were sold to the Duke of Portland, who, in about 1840, leased them to Herbert Greenhalgh. The house, in a public park, is now a hotel and the mill is home to a variety of small firms. The mill pond has been drained and filled in and the site is now occupied by apartments, having formerly been the premises of a car dealership.

Field Mill

In 1785 William Smith changed the use of the old corn mill at Field Mill to cotton spinning. By 1788 he was bought out by the Nottingham Hosiery group Stanfords, Elliott and Burnside. They spent about £1,000 on Field Mill to update it. In 1791 with the help of John Marker, they enlarged Field Mill dam, which forced the closure of Daniel Drury's corn mill upstream due to water back-ups. Since 1840 and for most of its working life the factory was occupied by Messrs Greenhalgh until it was demolished in the 1920s. The first picture shows Field Mill and the mill pond in the 1920s, with the master's house on the right. The factory was demolished before 1925. The second picture shows the enormous 40ft diameter water wheel in the 1920s before it was demolished. The master's house is still here and is now a public house, and the mill dam is a favourite fishing haunt.

Mill dam 1950

Mill dam 1985

Bath Mill

This is a Grade II listed building that has fallen on hard times. There has been a great deal of vandalism due to the mill being unoccupied for a good many years. Built in 1792 and situated on the corner of Bath Lane and Sandy Lane, near to the site of the old spring-fed public bathing pool from which it takes its name, the mill was able to take advantage of the power from the River Maun and produced thread for the Nottingham lacemakers until Messrs Goldie, Wade and Goldie used it for hosiery manufacturing from 1885. They left in 1985 and the mill became increasingly derelict. This building has now been demolished after further acts of vandalism.

Hermitage Mill

A fine 18th-century building, now being restored and converted, Hermitage Mill was built by Samuel Unwin and James Heygate in 1782 for cotton spinning, on a site leased from the Duke of Portland. It was one of five mills using water power along the Maun financed by the Duke of Portland in an effort to alleviate Mansfield's economic depression in the late 18th century. In 1835 a bankrupt Heygate leased the mill to James Fisher, a London lace maker, who, with the Alcock family, made lace thread. Samuel Eden, from 1860 to 1932, were the last occupiers of the mill to use it for hosiery manufacturing. The site had been a mill since 1302, at that time under Thomas Beck the Bishop of St Davids, and has had a variety of owners, lately a builders' merchants. Now, with the mill having been vacated, it is being restored, minus the rather ugly later additions, as a Grade II listed building.

Old Town Mill

This mill, on Bridge Street, is situated on the River Maun as it flows under the road. It was, in 1744, newly erected as a corn and malt mill, probably under the ownership of Geoffrey Smith. By 1784 William Smith, quite likely Geoffrey's son, was offering the milling equipment for sale and began negotiations with the Duke of Portland to change the mill into a cotton spinning one using water power to drive the machinery. He also began a Sunday school so that his young employees could learn the basics in literacy and numeracy as well as religious values. Smith also owned Field Mill. In 1788 Smith was bought out by the Stamfords, Elliott and Burnside Partnership. They sold Town Mill to John Hancock and Francis Wakefield of Nottingham, but by 1830 Town Mill had been bought by John Bradley, who later built New Town Mill. It was in use until 1907 when it partially burnt down, but it has since been renovated and reopened as a public house.

New Town Mill

The New Town Mill, Ratcliffe Gate, was so-called because the firm's founder, John Bradley (who started his business in Nottingham in 1827), had owned the 'Old' Town Mill since the 1830s. It was built in 1870 for his successors, M.G. & A. Bradley, whose firm was later amalgamated with the Fine Cotton Spinners & Doublers' Association. It was steam-powered with 22,000 spindles, and at its peak employed about 1,000 people. It ceased operation in about 1956 and remained derelict for decades before being demolished in 1987.

Lawn Mills, Walkden Street

Lawn Mills was built as a cotton-doubling mill in 1906 for John Harwood Cash, a descendant of Mary Cash, who had founded the business in Portland Mill, Victoria Street, in 1839. The firm was very successful, and by the time it was taken over by Courtaulds in 1973 the annual turnover was around £15 million and the total number of employees was about 1,000. The takeover was not a success, however, and Lawn Mills was closed within a few years. It reopened in 1984 as the Rosemary Centre.

Interior view c.1970

'Buster' Linney, son-in-law of John Harwood Cash, is the central figure in the 1950 photograph below.

Interior view 1910

Portland Mill, Victoria Street
Portland Mill on Victoria Street was founded by Mary Cash and family in 1839 and was the first steam-powered cotton-doubling mill in the town. The family prospered and remained in business for many years, establishing Lawn Mills in 1906.

Notable Buildings

Gilcroft

Gilcroft was a large house standing in its own grounds, which were bounded by Midworth Street (formerly Blind Lane), Brunt Street and Church Lane. Built c.1790, it was the home of William Brodhurst, owner of the old Maltings on Blind Lane. Later in the 19th century it passed on to Samuel Midworth, an iron founder who carried on his business in Leeming Street, on the site of what is now the old library and museum. An interesting, if apocryphal, little story about him survives. The Market Place was cleared to its present extent by about 1840. In 1849, however, the monument to Lord George Bentinck was erected in the middle. Samuel did not approve. It had been his daily habit to walk from his home to his iron foundry via Brunt Street, Albert Street, Market Street, across the Market Place and up Leeming Street. When the monument was erected, Samuel vowed never to enter the Market Place again. He kept his word. He had a gate made near the junction of Blind Lane and Church Lane and thereafter walked through this down Church Lane, turned the corner onto Bridge Street, then walked up Toothill Lane to Leeming Street. The house survived until 1904, when the house and gardens were sold off and the area was redeveloped. Today, St Peter's Way cuts through the middle of what was the estate.

Town Hall, Market Place

The town hall was built between 1835 and 1836 by the Town Hall Company, which raised £6,000 for the purpose via £50 shares. The foundation stone was laid by Mr John Coke of Debdale Hall on 21 July 1835, and the town hall opened the following year. As well as an assembly room, offices, reading room, etc., the hall also included a 10-cell lock-up and police accommodation in the rear. In 1837 it also installed a public clock, illuminated by gas supplied by the Mansfield Gas Light Company. Semi-circular railings were provided in the front, but these were removed when the Bentinck Memorial was erected to compensate for the loss of space in the newly opened Market Place. The Town Commissioners (the forerunners of the local council) used to rent out rooms for their meetings, until in 1885 they purchased the hall from the Town Hall Company.

Market Place.					Mansfield.

Moot Hall

The Moot Hall was where the townspeople, or rather those who were eligible to have a say, met to discuss the business of the town. The ground floor was open and was used for the storage of market furniture. It was rebuilt in local stone at the expense of Lady Henrietta Cavendish of Oxford and Mortimer, who was 'lord of the manor' in 1752. It is said that after a brief look at the building she returned to her carriage to be driven back to Welbeck, having decided she did not approve. In the early part of the 19th century the open ground floor was enclosed and became shops. At one time Mrs Gordon had her drapery business there, and later a boot and shoe shop called Messrs Smith and Brown had premises there. The upper floors were used extensively for town meetings and assemblies, which were the high spots of the local social calendar. These assemblies were usually held during the time of the full moon to help light the journey of the people attending. In 1921 it became the Yorkshire Penny Bank, later the Yorkshire Bank. This has now moved to newer premises in Westgate and the building is another group of shops. The upper storeys have no known use. It is said that the stone not used in the building of the Moot Hall was used to build Waverley House in Westgate.

Lime Tree Place, Ratcliffe Gate, c.1900
Tudor in origin, the house, particularly the windows, had alterations dating from the Georgian period. Behind the house were the brewhouse, stables, paddocks and a garden that extended across the River Maun to Scotland Close on Lister Lane, now part of Church Side. It is reputed to have been the early home of Richard Sterne, who was educated at the grammar school, entered the church and rose to become Archbishop of Canterbury. In the 18th century it became the home of the Burden family, manufacturers of thread and cotton. H.S. Shacklock, formerly cashier and later (1885–99) partner in the Mansfield Brewery, was one of the later occupants. Lime Tree place was partly demolished c.1903 when the refuse destructor and power station was opened. This used water from the River Maun for generating steam. The remaining buildings were demolished in 1971 to make way for the Electricity Board offices.

Tudor House, Stockwell Gate, c.1970
Tudor House was situated on the south side, a little higher up than the Co-operative store. This photograph was taken in 1892 and shows two of the businesses at that time. In the foreground are G. Richardson, tin and copperplate worker and William Hough, general store. The entrance led to other Tudor properties in Woodcock's Yard which were demolished in a clearance of old properties in the 1920s. One the left-hand side, at the base of Mr Hough's shop, is an old milestone that reads 'Alfreton 9 miles'.

The opening on the far left led to Woodcock's Yard, where W.H. Lee and Sons had their printing works. Baby Fayre had their shop in the former Tudor house and access at the side was called Chapel Yard. This led to the rear of the Crown Hostelry and the Meridian hosiery factory. In earlier times it possibly led to the Quaker Meeting House or the former Congregational Chapel that was opposite. The whole of this property, as far back as Quaker Lane, was demolished in 1974 when Quaker Way was constructed.

Walkden House, Stockwell Gate
This illustration is a photograph of a watercolour by A.S. Buxton, who was also probably the photographer. Walkden House was built in the early 19th century by Mr S. Unwin of Sutton and later occupied by Mr W. Walkden, a well-known solicitor. Walkden Street was named after him, as were the buildings (seen below) on Stockwell Gate, photographed by Mr Purdy in 1969. When Walkden House was demolished and the surrounding area redeveloped, the site was used for the Tesco supermarket (now closed), with parking facilities above.

Interior of Ravenscroft, Crow Hill Drive

Home of Albert Sorby Buxton (1869–1932)

A. S. Buxton's interest in art led to him becoming headmaster of the School of Art, with which he was associated for over 30 years. This, after many changes of location, was finally housed behind the new technical college on Chesterfield Road. It was at Ravenscroft that he painted many of his pictures, including those of historic Mansfield which are now on display in the Buxton Room at the museum. With his enthusiasm to share the past of his home town, he became a founder member (1918) of the Old Mansfield Society and its first secretary. He also wrote, and illustrated, two books on the history of the town in the 18th and 19th centuries. Among his other interests were photography (founder member of the first Photographic Society), music (he helped start the Amateur Operatic Society) and golf (a member first of the Ravensdale and later the Sherwood Forest clubs). He also designed the town's World War One Memorial which stands in Carr Bank.

Old Summer House (between Church Street and Toothill Lane)
Many of the properties on the eastern side of Church Street were built into the sandstone rock. On the higher ground above, which ran parallel with Toothill Lane, gardens were made to cultivate vegetables, fruit and flowers. This summer house, directly above one of the houses, was once a feature of the owner's garden, which became a car park later in the 20th century.

Bath House, Bath Lane

When Bath House was first built, c.1795, it would have stood alone on the outskirts of the town and had extensive views of the countryside. These were blocked in the 1870s when the Midland Railway line was opened, and gradually other properties were built around it. The bay windows were probably added in the 20th century, when the ground floor was converted into offices. At one time it was the office of the Deputy Registrar of Births, Deaths and Marriages and was later occupied by the Co-operative Insurance Society. Bath House was demolished in the 1970s to make a pull-in for buses.

The Rock Houses on Rock Hill were hollowed out of outcrops of sandstone or limestone to provide primitive homes. Most had a fireplace and chimney and water was collected in outside butts. Traditionally, families of besom makers, who also furnished the constabulary with birch rods, lived in these dingy, unhealthy dwellings. They collected the birch from nearby Ling Forest, by permission of the Duke of Portland, and were exempt from local taxes. Mr John Bramwell (1815–1900) is here seen outside his house in the 1890s. His widow, Charlotte, lived here until about 1910. It was the last rock house to be occupied.

Waverley House, Westgate

Waverley House was built in 1753, reputedly from stone left over from the building of the Moot Hall in the Market Place. Unlike the adjoining Barrett's Sports and Leather Goods shop, and all the other properties as far down Westgate as the Granada cinema, it was spared demolition when the Four Seasons shopping centre was built in 1972. Similarly, the buildings behind Waverley House, such as Sherwood Printers on Meeting House Lane, were also demolished in 1972.

The Ridge, in the Park Conservation Area, was one of many prestigious houses built in this once exclusive part of the town. The estate is to the north of Carr Bank Park, which was a desirable area where businessmen were able to live in well-built residences, conveniently close to the town centre. The Ridge was designed by Robert Frank Vallance as his family home. He was surveyor and architect for Mansfield Town Council after 1891 and before that for the town's commissioners. Saved from demolition by means of a public inquiry in 2002, it experienced the usual vandalism while remaining empty.

Berry Hill Hall was built in the 1750s for William Bilbie, but has been extensively enlarged and remodelled by subsequent owners, who included Sir Edward Walker (1799–1874), who was High Sheriff of Nottinghamshire in 1866–67, and William Hollins, owner of the Pleasley Vale Mills. In 1924 it became a rehabilitation and convalescent home for injured miners and was subsequently incorporated into the property of the National Health Service, where it remained until 1988 when it was sold off to a builder by the local health authority. Despite its Grade II listed status, the house remained empty and suffered much vandalism for several years until it was sold on again to a developer who is currently turning the property into luxury apartments. The park, however, remains the property of the Coal Industry Social Welfare Organisation (CISWO) and is maintained by the District Council.

The Sun Parlour from Croquet Lawn, Miners Welfare Convalescent Home, Berry Hill Hall, Mansfield. Empire View. 0164.5.

Carr Bank

A Grade II listed building, the house was built in 1805 for Charles Stanton, a cotton spinner who owned Stanton Mill on Bath Lane. The architect was William Wilkinson of The Priory, Mansfield Woodhouse. Charles Stanton later sold both the house and the mill to the 4th Duke of Portland. Between 1836 and 1907 the house was occupied by the Greenhalgh family. They were cotton doublers who, at the height of their commercial prosperity in the mid-19th century, employed about 600 people (mostly women) in three mills in the town – Stanton Mill, Little Matlock Mill and Field Mill. Throughout most of World War One the house was let to John Plowright Houfton, managing director of the Bolsover Colliery Co. Ltd, which at that time was developing the Mansfield (Crown Farm), Rufford and Clipstone Collieries. After World War One, the 6th Duke of Portland sold the house and grounds to Mansfield Borough Council for about half its market value. The house was converted into council offices (initially housing the School of Art), while the grounds were opened as a public park. The war memorial on the right of the picture below was unveiled on 4 August 1924 and dedicated to the men of Mansfield who gave their lives during World War One by the Bishop of Southwell. In 1987 the house was closed when the new Civic Centre on Chesterfield Road South was opened, and in 1989 it (though not the grounds) was sold and converted into a hotel and restaurant.

Westgate House, Parson's Yard, Westgate

A description written in 1921 says that Westgate House was stone-built and partly of Elizabethan origin, with oak beams and cellars with natural rock floors. Two staircases led to the upper floors past windows which had been blocked up when the window tax, first levied in 1686, was in force. The top storey had concrete floors laid on reeds, and in the water-cistern chamber wattle and daub filling could be seen between the beams.

Gilcroft Chambers, junction of Gilcroft Street and Church Lane
Gilcroft Chambers was designed by F.W. Tempest. It was a local government building, housing the Registrar of Births, Deaths and Marriages, the Pest Control offices and the Health Department. The building, and most of Gilcroft Street, was demolished to make way for St Peter's Way in 1970.

Goodacre Estate
The first prefabricated dwelling to be erected in Mansfield at the end of World War Two stood on the Goodacre Estate off Pelham Street. Furnished by Mr W.A. Symington of the Co-operative Central Store, a crowd of interested persons assembled for the opening. Subsequently faced in brick, some still remain in use.

RECREATION

Titchfield Park is Mansfield's oldest public park. In the mid-19th century an area of swampy land in Mansfield dissected by the River Maun was drained and began to be used by local people for informal recreation and fairs. The Duke of Portland leased the land to the Improvement Commissioners on low terms for the creation of a Public Recreational Park in 1879. By the 1880s further improvements were made to the site, creating a more formal pleasure ground, including the construction of a bandstand and planting of an avenue of trees. By 1914 a paddling pool and bowling green had been added and that year the park was handed over by the Duke of Portland (when his son, the Marquis of Titchfield, came of age) to the Mansfield Corporation and named Titchfield Park. The park has suffered through vandalism and lack of development (although improvements have been made with the building of the Water Meadows swimming baths). The Heritage Lottery Fund is to give a £983,000 grant for the restoration of Titchfield Park, contributing towards a £1.3 million package of improvements.

WILD'S THEATRE
White Hart Croft, Mansfield.

NOVELTY! NOVELTY!! NOVELTY!!!

FIRST NIGHT OF THE SPLENDID DRAMA ENTITLED

CLAUDE DUVAL!!!

THE LADIES HIGHWAYMAN

First Night of the MOST LAUGHABLE of all FARCES entitled

DICK TURPIN.

Saturday Evening, Feb. 4th, 1860,

The performance will commence with the Powerful Drama, in 3 acts, produced under the directions
of Mr. J. C. Donnelly, entitled

CLAUDE
DUVAL!!

The LADIES HIGHWAYMAN,

OR, THE

MURDER AT THE LONE HOUSE

CLAUDE

DUVAL

DICK

TURPIN.

Charles the Second......Mr SMITH.   Colonel Blood......Mr J. C. DONNELLY.   Mervyn.........Mr KEEFE.
Claude Duval, (the Ladies Highwayman)................................Mr MACGUINNESS.
Titus Oates....................Mr TOMKINSON.   Sir Edmundbery Godfrey.....................Mr DELAFIELD.
Peter Prance, a carpenter...Mr HEWITT.   Bedeon...Mr PALMER.   Earl of Rochester...Mr LAWRENCE.
Elkanak, a Jew..Mr ELLIS JONES.
Lady Howard...............Mrs MACGUINNESS.   Aurora Sydney.......Mrs J. C. DONNELLY.

This 1860 theatre poster is a reminder of the days of travelling showmen and theatrical troupes who would stay for five or six months during the winter, giving nightly performances in tents. White Hart Croft was on the site of Dame Flogan Street.

Mansfield Public Library, Leeming Street
The laying of the foundation stone took place on 6 July 1904, and the library was officially opened on 24 May 1905. The building was erected using money donated by Andrew Carnegie (£3,500) on land given by the Duke of Portland (c.800 square yards). A second storey was added in February 1932 to house the Reference Section. The building was closed in March 1977 (when the library moved to new premises in Westgate), until November 1978, when the triple Action Theatre Group leased the building from Nottinghamshire County Council. As a result of losing Arts Council grants, the theatre group were unable to renew their lease in April 1981 and moved out. The building remained unoccupied until October 1982, when the Mansfield Community Arts Centre was established. It is now, somewhat confusingly, known as the Old Library.

Winifred, Duchess of Portland, was a generous and hardworking benefactress to Mansfield. She and her husband, the 6th duke, worked to establish the now-demolished Harlow Wood Hospital and the Portland Training College on land given for free by the duke. Her love of animals led her to figure prominently in the campaign to ban the wearing of osprey feathers in hats, and she frequently stopped her car if she saw an animal in distress or an overladen horse on the country roads. In July 1939, heedless of the gathering clouds of war, the golden wedding anniversary of the Ducal couple was celebrated with a pageant depicting scenes from the past of Welbeck Abbey. Mansfield's episode in this depicted the visit in 1633 of Charles I and Queen Henrietta Maria, who were entertained by a masque by Ben Johnson. The weather was inclement and the long dresses of some ladies concealed wellington boots.

On with the show, the first musical in technicolor, was the first feature when the Granada cinema on Westgate was opened in 1930, though it was then called the Plaza. It was renamed the Granada in 1947. With a seating capacity of 1,550, it was the largest cinema in the town, and also incorporated a much-appreciated restaurant. There were major alterations in 1935 and 1936, which saw the introduction of lavatories, a stage and also the 'mighty' Wurlitzer organ. Live shows were introduced during the 1960s to boost attendances and the acts included Billy Fury, Joe Brown, Cliff Richard and even the Beatles (though the latter were a supporting act to the then more famous Helen Shapiro). Unfortunately, its location coincided with that of the major re-development that resulted in the Four Seasons shopping centre, and it was demolished in 1973, closing with the film Young Winston. The Wurlitzer organ was rescued, however, and now has a new home in Matlock, Derbyshire. The site was then occupied first by the Littlewoods department store and currently by Primark.

Chronicle Advertiser, 21 February 1963

The Cantamus Girls' Choir celebrating their 25th anniversary in 1993. The choir, founded by Pamela Cook MBE in 1968, is simply the best girls' choir in the world, having won numerous first prizes in prestigious competitions at home and abroad. They have represented Great Britain at events in East and West Europe, Israel, Canada, US and Japan. In 2004 and 2006 they were awarded a World Choir Olympics Championship and two gold medals. Over the years, and always under the directorship of Pamela Cook, the girls have sung with leading orchestras, commissioned works from renowned composers, been featured on TV and radio and made several CDs. Many former members have gone on to have successful careers in music.

The Hippodrome

The Hippodrome on Midworth Street was built in 1906 as a music hall. The original owner was Bertie Oaksford of Sutton-in-Ashfield. It received a cinema licence in 1913 and live shows finished about six years later following alterations, in which 12 small boxes were removed and tip-up seating installed. It became part of the Granada group around 1950, was renamed the Century and used for bingo sessions in 1962. Following a disastrous fire it was demolished in 1991.

The Picturedrome on Belvidere Street was originally built and owned by Antonio Richardson in 1920 and used as a silent movie cinema with orchestra. It lasted as a full-time cinema until 1924 and part-time until 1928. It had a chequered history until it reopened in 1934 as the Queen's Theatre, showing local variety and music hall acts, but it closed again in December 1935. In 1941 it became a British restaurant, and after World War Two it was used for offices. Currently unoccupied, it was last used as a local dancing school.

Originally opened as The Grand Theatre in 1906, it was modernised in 1928 and operated mainly as a cinema thereafter, but with occasional runs of stage entertainments. It was bought by the ABC company in 1930 but was not renamed until 1963. In 1978 it became a triple cinema but closed in 1997 when the multiplex cinema opened off Nottingham Road. It is now a snooker hall.

Mansfield Leisure Centre, officially opened on 21 September 1980 by Frankie Vaughan, was a facility provided and maintained jointly by Nottinghamshire County Council and Mansfield District Council. This joint venture cost £700,000 and was opened for business on 1 July 1980. The general public and schools both made extensive use of the badminton, squash and table tennis facilities, while at other times the centre was used for activities as varied as wrestling, keep-fit, martial arts, antique fairs and concerts. Along with an adjacent car dealership and other businesses, it was demolished in 2007 and replaced by a Tesco supermarket.

Mansfield's first public baths were erected on the banks of the Maun in Littleworth in 1853. The architect was Charles Neale and the builder Charles Lindley, a quarry owner and builder of the Bentinck Monument. When first opened, the establishment was well patronised by local people and those from surrounding districts. A welcome improvement was made when heat from the adjacent foundry was used to heat the large pool. Enlarged in 1904, the Baths continued in use until 1990, when the site was cleared to become part of the car park for the new Water Meadows Leisure Centre.

There was little concern for animal welfare in 1890, when these bears were put through a performance by their gypsy handlers. A sizeable crowd has gathered to watch, mainly composed of children, almost all wearing caps. In the background on the right is Crampton and Clements auctioneers' office in a building designed by Mansfield-born architect Watson Fothergill. On the left is Dr Tate's house and surgery.

The Austin Racing Sevens, with Lord Austin on the right, in 1923 for the Clipstone speed trials held on Clipstone Drive, or Duke's Drive. This was a long, straight, private road, which can still be walked today. The road and Cavendish Lodge were owned by the Duke of Portland, a keen enthusiast.

Before the formation of Mansfield Town Football Club there were several local clubs, many of which owed their existence to local churches. One such club Mansfield Methodist FC, are pictured here in a team photograph for 1911–12. The two main teams of the town around the turn of the 19th century were the Mansfield Mechanics and the Mansfield Wesleyans, and it was the latter team, which had been founded in 1897, that were renamed Mansfield Town FC in 1910. The club's most famous result to date was the 3–0 defeat of West Ham in the third round of the FA Cup in 1969. At that time West Ham were in the First Division and fielded World Cup-winning players such as Martin Peters, Geoff Hurst and, of course, the captain Bobby Moore.

Mansfield Town won the Notts FA Senior Cup in the 1922–23 season with a 2–1 victory over Newark Athletic at Sutton Town's ground.

Spectators at Field Mill in 1923.

The new West Stand, October 2000.

The new North Stand, October 2000.

The new South Stand, October 2000.

The Field Mill stadium was rebuilt during 2000 and 2001, with new North, South and West Stands. The above photograph shows the ground being officially reopened by the Deputy Prime Minister John Prescott MP in July 2001.

STREETS

The junction of Berry Hill Road with Kate Moody Lane (Windsor Road) and Bottle Lane (Forest Road) is shown here in 1933. This area was in the process of development and being advertised as desirable housing in a healthy area. The central house is 1A Berry Hill Road, with fields behind and a few dwellings on the future Windsor Road. The row of cottages on the left horizon are still there, but the thick hedge that appears to block the road has long since gone. On the extreme right of the picture the pine tree indicating the position of Limmers Farm further up Berry Hill Road can just be seen.

Ladybrook Estate

In the aftermath of World War Two, Mansfield faced a housing crisis. Domestic building had ceased in 1940 and a burgeoning population needed homes. In 1947 the council acquired land for the Ladybrook Estate, named from the stream that rose in Cumberland's field. Brick Kiln Lane, so named from an early industrial activity, is one of the main thoroughfares in the estate. By 1952, 1,270 council houses had been built. Many are now privately owned.

Brick Kiln Lane in 1947...

…and in 1986.

Meadow Row, Littleworth

This row of stone-built cottages were inhabited by workers in the adjacent Meadow Foundry established in 1852. When Mansfield Baths were built in 1854, waste heat from the Foundry was piped to heat the large pool. The business changed hands several times and for a time was used as a tobacco factory. The buildings were vacated in 1960 and eventually demolished. The cottages, which had lost part of their gardens to the Great Central Railway line, were pulled down at the same time.

Architectural conceits

The first photograph shows the Leeming Street post office, once occupied by Syd Dernley who had been an assistant hangman to Albert Pierrepoint. To the right of the post office are two shops with apparent 'magpie' half-timbering. However, all is not as it seems, as this was simply decorative, a popular addition in the 1920s to create a picturesque effect. Other examples of this could be seen in Toothill Lane, Leeming Street and Church Street.

Belvedere Street

The centre of the first picture shows Stainforth's shop and residence. No. 45a was occupied by the family from 1882 with their shop being established in 1883. The 1891 census has the family consisting of Edward Simeon Stainforth and his wife Sarah, three children, Johanna, George and William, and Annie Marsh, who was a boarder, all living there. The Belle View Inn, which can be seen on the extreme left of the second picture, was built in 1880 and demolished to make way for road-widening in 1981. Belvedere Street has had many varied small businesses, mostly short-lived, such as, in about 1800, the William Billingsley porcelain-painting business. In the first picture can be seen the rear entrance to Henshaw, a prestigious furniture firm still trading today, and the tall building at the back is the Courtaulds factory, now demolished. A little alleyway called Quaker Lane joined Belvedere Street to Queen's Street, which has now gone, as has the elegant 18th-century Quaker Meeting House.

Church Street

Above is an 1884 photograph of Church Street, or Kirk (Church) Gate as it had been called previously. All the street, from the bow-fronted shop on the left down to the church, was owned by the Southwell Chantry and leased by the vicar and churchwardens of Mansfield. In 1884–85 the land was sold to the town's Improvement Commissioners, who redeveloped the area on its present lines. The shop on the extreme left became the ironmongers Blake and Beeley, the bow-fronted shop was a saddler's shop and next to it was the entrance to White Lion Yard and the pub of the same name. The photo below was taken in 1900. On the right is the Swan Hotel, in the previous century a renowned posting inn, while on the left is the jewellers Martin and Wilkinson, a prestigious firm still operating today.

Lurchills

The Lurchills was an alley that connected Woodhouse Road with Westgate, via Clumber Street. Vagrants were expected to take this route to avoid the town centre. From Westgate they were to go via Meetinghouse Lane to Rosemary Street and thus to Stockwell Gate and their presumed destination, the Workhouse. A part of the Lurchills still remains – the link between Clumber Street and Westgate. The photograph here shows a part of the Lurchills on the north side of Clumber Street in 1970, before it disappeared in a redevelopment, while below it is a 1972 photograph of the still-existing entrance to the Lurchills alleyway on Westgate.

St John Street

As Mansfield grew it was decided that a new church and school were needed on the north side of the town. Catlow Street was chosen and renamed St John Street. Catlow Street, a narrow, semi-rural lane, had largely been purchased by Revd Catlow, who had a school in Cromwell House, Westgate. The church, costing £8,000, was built from local stone in an Early Decorated Style between 1854–56 by Mr H.I. Stevens, with money provided by H. Galley Knight, a Warsop man, to the tune of £6,000, with the Duke of Portland and the potential parishioners donating £1,000 a piece. It was consecrated by the Bishop of Lincoln, the Right Reverend John Jackson (1811–1885), on 29 July 1856. The school opened in 1862 with the first headmaster a Mr Columbine and served the community for 140 years before Southwell Diocese closed it. The first photograph comes from the Pelham Postcard Collection produced by Boots in 1915. The second one shows a modern view taken in 1971 by Mr Purdy.

St. John's Street, Mansfield.

Ratcliffe Gate

Ratcliffe Gate in 1914 and 1970. It is readily seen to be a residential street and much narrower than in 1970. Ratcliffe Gate is one of the main streets leading east from the town up a long hill, at the top of which were the Rock Houses, built just outside the town's jurisdiction making them exempt from taxes. At the top of the hill were two windmills: Abraham's and Rock Mill (though the latter had been called Jackson's and Club at various times). There were several mills in a line along the hill running roughly along the eastern edge of town.

Stockwell Gate

The 1970s and 1980s were the 'years of construction' in Mansfield. This is a picture of Stockwell Gate and shows Tesco and the car park above the shop being constructed. Beyond Tesco is the new bus station. In the foreground is the bridge over Stockwell Gate, which carries Quaker Way, so-called because it replaced the 18th-century Meeting House situated on Quaker Lane and marks the Quaker Heritage of Mansfield. The bridge was open for use in November 1974 and acts as an inner ring road for Mansfield. In 2007 Tesco relocated to Chesterfield Road South and the bus station is now due to be relocated.

St Peter's Way

These pictures show the early construction of St Peter's Way in 1972. The top picture shows the junction with the top of Leeming Street, with what was to be a bus stand on the left and the ABC cinema (now Riley's snooker hall) on the right. The lower picture shows the gasometer, which was demolished in 1975, and to the left of the gasometer is Bradley's Mill, which was demolished in 1988. At one time Bradley's Mill had 1,000 workers. The first part of St Peter's Way, uphill from Bridge Street to Nottingham Road, is virtually complete. The very muddy part seen in the foreground goes from Bridge Street up to the top of Leeming Street, past, on the right of the picture, the Methodist Day School, which was built in 1821 and was the first purpose-built Sunday school in Mansfield. This served as a day school too, giving some of Mansfield's children a rudimentary education. It was considered important enough to have a Preservation Order attached to it.

Sadler's Court, Stockwell Gate

A row of timber-framed cottages and the entrance to Sadler's Court photographed in 1870. They were pulled down and replaced by a town house in 1880. The entrance to the court was retained and is now used as a gated entrance to a car park for Lloyds Trustees Bank employees. Jackson's chemist, in the photograph below, occupied an early 19th-century building, which was replaced by a 1960s concrete structure.

Leeming Street
Beard and Freeman, corn and seed merchants, 1962. The large gateway leads to the rear of the Green Dragon, seen in the picture opposite. The Green Dragon was built in 1800, and a building in the back (on the right of the lower picture opposite) was opened as the Tivoli Music Hall in the 1880s until the licence was removed in 1909 following police complaints regarding the degrading nature of the performances and drunken audiences (the price of admission included a free glass of beer). The music hall was later converted into a billiard room containing six full-sized tables. In 1910 the landlord, Harry Scarlett, entered a cage containing five lions during the Bostock and Wombwell Menagerie's visit to Mansfield Market Place. The building was closed in the 1960s and eventually demolished for shop development in 1969–70.

TRADE AND INDUSTRY

The Cattle Market on Nottingham Road was opened in 1878, replacing the previous practice of holding stock auctions by the old Market Cross on Westgate. The land was known previously as the water meadows, and the old name was thought appropriate for the new swimming baths that opened on the site in 1990.

Sanderson's Foundry on Leeming Street was originally started by Samuel Midworth at the beginning of the 19th century. By the 1870s it had passed to C. & F. Sanderson (former apprentices at James Maude), and later became known as Sanderson & Robinson. It was forced to move out in 1903 on the expiry of its lease from the Duke of Portland, who then donated the land for the establishment of the public library and museum. Sanderson & Robinson moved first to Hermitage Lane in 1903 and then in 1930 to Sheepbridge Lane. It was bought out by the Meadow Foundry Co. in 1957, though retained its separate identity for another 20 years.

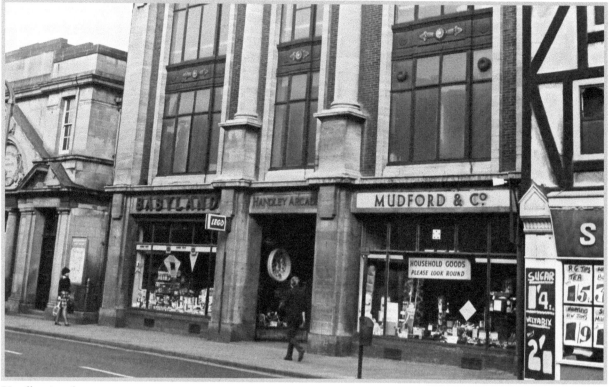

Handley Arcade

The Handley Arcade was built in 1927 as an early version of a shopping mall with 15 shops. It is an L-shaped building with the most imposing entrance shown above on Leeming Street, and the other entrance, shown below, around the corner on Toothill Lane. The architects were the local firm of Cook, Howard & Lane, and the Leeming Street façade was constructed with a steel frame faced with Mansfield and Ancaster stone.

Sergeant Pearson with local character 'Tubby' Machin in the cattle market in 1900. The land for the cattle market on Nottingham Road was purchased by the Town Commissioners (forerunners of the Borough, later District, Council) from the Duke of Portland and opened in 1878. Previously the cattle market was held on Westgate.

Water Meadow's Horsefair

The horsefairs always took place on the Water Meadows between Nottingham Road and Littleworth in the third week of July to coincide with the July Fair, which was held in the Market Place. The horsefairs ceased in the 1930s. Before World War One the horse was the main method of transport and Mansfield had its full complement of saddlers, one of whom had his business where the China Basket is now. In 1914 the Duke of Portland presented the area to Mansfield to mark the coming-of-age of his son and heir the Marquis of Titchfield and his own Silver Wedding Celebrations, thus the park is now known as Titchfield Park. Adjacent to it was the cattle market purchased from the Duke of Portland at 2s 6d (12.5p) a yard. This solved the problem of animals, previously sold at the top of Westgate by the Old Market Cross and, after 1870, in the Market place, where, on occasions, beasts had run amok and damaged both premises and people.

The Mansfield Shoe Company
The Mansfield Shoe Company on the corner of Stockwell Gate and Dallas Street began life as Royce, Gascoigne & Co. in 1871. The Dallas Street premises, shown here, date from about 1900 and at one time employed about 700 people, but following various financial ups and downs, finally closed in 2004. The building was demolished in 2006.

Interior view 1909 of The Mansfield Shoe Company.

The Mansfield & Sutton Cooperative Society built a store on Stockwell Gate in 1865 (top). It was destroyed by a fire in 1918 but was replaced by the larger store in 1922 (bottom left), which still exists, though it was greatly remodelled in the 1960s (bottom right) and is no longer a Co-operative Society store.

The Co-op Superstore on Station Street was opened in 1984 but was never a commercial success and closed 12 years later. It did not remain an empty shell for long, however, as it was razed to the ground soon after it closed, and the site became incorporated into the St Peter's Retail Park.

The Mansfield & Worksop Co-operative Dairy, Southwell Road West, was opened in 1950 but closed and was demolished in 1983 due to coal mining subsidence. The site is now occupied partly by Adams Way, opposite the junction of Oak Tree Lane and Southwell Road West.

Quarrying was one of the town's oldest industries, the fine Magnesium Limestone being used in the construction of most of the buildings locally and also in part of the Houses of Parliament. The photograph shows a block of stone being transported from the Chesterfield Road quarry of Thomas Millott, a builder, mason and quarry owner who lived on Belmont Terrace around the mid-1880s.

Mansfield's first telephone exchange was opened in 1889 by the National Telephone Company. The office was set up at 49 West Gate in a building used by other firms. Few people subscribed to the service in the early years, and a degree of hostility was shown to the telephone poles in the streets. Subscribers in 1899 were dissatisfied, but the service gradually flourished as businessmen realised the benefits of rapid communication with customers. In the photograph the central lady is Mrs Harrington, the manageress, who was in overall charge in the early 1900s.

Chapman's cycle shop stood on Stockwell Gate by the junction with Bancroft Lane, near to the Red Lion Hotel. In this photograph, from 1912, bicycles have been moved outside to show off the stock, no doubt to be taken back into the premises later. A sharp eye had to be kept on the tyres hanging within reach of potential thieves, a danger pointed out to shopkeepers by the police, who warned that this practice was an open invitation.

At A & C Sports in 1988 no such items were displayed outside. The stock is 'high-tech' of its period, mainly racing cycles and accessories. Behind the counter is Dale Marchant, assistant to Cyril Harper, the proprietor. This shop stood just below the Red Lion.

Miss Lily Wright worked as an assistant in the Littleworth Newsagents, almost opposite to her home on St Andrews Terrace. Here she was about 16 years old, in 1928. The shop sold many items – chocolates, sweets, tobacco and household goods. The shop is still a newsagents, with the same steep steps, but it no longer has a sunblind or the letter box bearing the initials of Edward VII.

George Ellis began his photography business, known as the Sherwood Photographic Company, in 1895, in premises on West Gate. At street level was the shop, where artists' materials, equipment for amateur photographers and a wide selection of postcards showing local beauty spots were on sale. The first floor held the technical apparatus, developing processes and darkroom, while the top floor was the studio glass house, a structure necessary in a period when electric lighting was not dependable. A serious fire in 1927 gutted the premises and Mr Ellis removed to Albert Street, where his business continued until his death in 1934.

Mr J.C. Eadson of Eclipse Yard, West Gate, posed for this photograph with his prize-winning entry in the Carters Show in 1913. This was an annual event when judging took place in the Market Place. The photograph was taken in West Gate, showing a window of the Eclipse Inn, with Jolly's tobacconist, Stephenson's stationers and Pick's haberdashery in the background. Mr Eadson's phone number was Mansfield 64.

In 1823–24 the Mansfield Gas Light Company built the first gas manufacturing plant in Lime Tree Place, at a cost of about £5,000. It had one gasholder with a capacity of around 510 cubic metres. The original pipes were bored out of tree trunks and by 1876 there were 191 street lights. The early ones were on cast-iron pillars with glazed lanterns. On 1 February 1837 the clock in the new town hall was lit by gaslight, making it the first public building to be illuminated in this way. A new plant had been built in 1847, near the original site, and in 1878 the company was bought by the Mansfield Improvement Commissioners for £37,500. They expanded the plant and the services it provided to the town. On 6 November 1903 a sixth gasometer was opened by John Crampton, Mayor of the Borough of Mansfield. These huge metal containers rose and fell, keeping the gas under pressure at all times. With the advent of North Sea natural gas, coal gas production ceased and the gasometers became redundant and were demolished in 1975.

In 1839 the firm of Barringer & Co. took over Ellis's mustard mill in Rock Valley, a former limestone quarry. In 1873 they began to pack the mustard in decorative tin boxes, instead of the wooden ones originally used. These proved to be very popular and the company began making tins for other firms, building a new tin-plating factory to keep up with the demand. In 1892 they set up their own printing plant. Barringer, Wallis and Manners Co. Ltd, with 143 employees, was incorporated in 1895, with £30,000 capital. Two years later they purchased Oddicroft Mill in Sutton-in-Ashfield and a new building was opened in Rock Valley – a tour of this was included when King George and Queen Mary visited Mansfield in 1914. The premises were again extended in 1927. Historically, one of the more well-known illustrations designed for the tins were the 'Alice in Wonderland' series. Permission to include the designs had to be sought from the Revd Charles Dodgson (Lewis Carroll), who agreed providing the firm sent him 200 empty tins, which he could then give to his 'little friends'. This was done with each new design. Once, however, the firm incurred the wrath of the author when, in a spirit of mistaken generosity, they sent him the 200 tins filled with the biscuits! The good Revd was most displeased, not least because he did not care for the brand of biscuits, and it took a grovelling apology before he was sufficiently mollified to permit his characters to be once more displayed on the tins. In 1939 Barringer, Wallis and Manners became part of the Metal Box Company. In the 1990s this became a subsidiary of the Carnaud Metal Box Speciality Packaging. It is currently part of the Crown Speciality Packaging UK Group.

An 1870s-style advertisement

What a piece of charming ephemera! The advert below for the firm of Fish & Pye is one of the things that get thrown away as unimportant and yet so much can be found in them. For example at the top of the photograph you can see the line of windmills on the top of the rock face. There was a line of them from Kate Moody Lane (Windsor Road) to Ravensdale – some grinding corn, others malt. Some were post mills that were cheaper and relatively easily moved, while others were more 'traditional' tower mills. The vestibule of the Old Meeting House is panelled in oak from one of those post mills, and the oak dates from the reign of Queen Elizabeth I. Rock Valley started out as a quarry site but the lure of the power of the River Maun soon tempted industry to develop there. As can be seen in the advert, Fish & Pye were bobbin and wood-turners. Bobbins were used in both the cotton and the earlier wool industries. However, they also manufactured many agricultural wooden implements such as scythes, snaiths, handles for hayforks, rakes, shafts for carts, brooms and mops, and also sails!

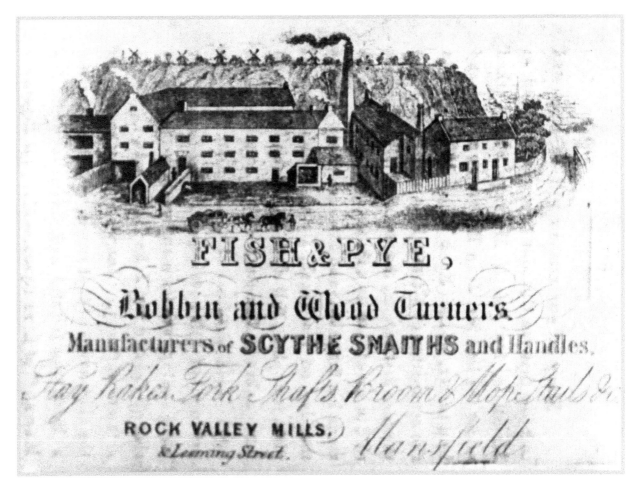

143

The Four Seasons Shopping Centre

The Four Seasons is a shopping centre with the town's library located over the top. These 1974 CHAD pictures taken during its construction show just how vast it is. It stretches roughly from near St Johns Street to Stockwell Gate and from Westgate to Quaker Way. The first draft plan was published in May 1963 and the completed building opened on 9 March 1976. The Old Mansfield Society has photographs of what was there before the Stockwell Gate Entrance – Caunt's Café, where one could get a strong cup of tea for 1d (½p), with soup for the same price. When the café was demolished it was found to have mediaeval origins. Four oaken crucks were found in two pairs, like upturned V's held together by a ridge beam going from one to the other. Unfortunately they were burnt before the museum could rescue them. The next-door inn, the King's Head, made, in some people's opinion, the best ham sandwiches in the town. In earlier days it had housed a boxing club and had had a lodging house on its premises as well as being a pub. Along Westgate many little alleyways and shops were demolished. The library entrance is roughly where Parson's Yard was. This housed Miss Parson's School, a private school for the young ladies and gentlemen of the town. It was a Tudor house, and rather spacious as far as we know.

Whiteley
The top picture shows the interior of Whiteley Electrical Radio Co., later Whiteley Electronics, on their Victoria Street premises. The firm was founded in 1926 by Alfred Whiteley, who had a starting capital of £350. His first factory was in the old Portland Cotton Mill on Victoria Street. Until 1970 they used old ex-army huts off Nottingham Road for storage and also, from 1936–70, the former skating rink and YMCA on Church Side as a cabinet-making factory. In 1970 a new factory was built on Quarry Lane and by the 1980s the firm was employing some 500 personnel. The second picture shows the Whiteley Boneham Company's mobile amplifier van for open-air broadcasting in 1928.

Supersave

The North Notts Newspaper picture of the construction of Mansfield's first supermarket, the Supersave Store in Church Street in the early 1970s. A shopper could enter the shop on Toothill Lane and, via an escalator, leave the store lower down on Church Street with all their shopping. As was common with the houses and shops down Church Street, the sandstone escarpment had been used to dig out caves either for storage or perhaps extra accommodation. Several caves were destroyed during the construction of Supersave, but there were opportunities for people to see them. A good example of caves are to be seen in White Lion Yard behind the steps leading to the car park in Toothill Lane.

Post Office, Church Street
In 1913 it was decided to build a main post office in Church Street. Below you can see the buildings before their demolition. Quite a few of the courts that Mansfield had in profusion, like Rose Court, Plough Court and Acton Court, went, the people and businesses being relocated. This is a 1906 photograph by A.S. Buxton.

Above is a 1972 photograph by Purdy. It is still very much in its original, ashlar stone, handsome state. On the extreme right is the former entrance to the rear. The architect's plans are still available today, and the style is Palladian.

Mansfield's stone quarries

Rich deposits of both limestone and sandstone lay beneath the surface of the land where Mansfield now stands, and it has been quarried from mediaeval times almost to the present day. Some of the stone was of such fine quality that it was used in building Southwell Minster and Nottingham Castle, though perhaps its best known and most prestigious use was in the 1839 rebuilding of the Houses of Parliament. Until the widespread use of brick in the second half of the 19th century, most of the houses in the town were built from local stone, and a fair number of them still survive. Work was hard in Mansfield's quarries and mechanical aids were few. Even the cranes in the 19th-century view of Rock Valley quarry below were manually operated. Personal safety was little regarded. None of the men are wearing hard hats or other forms of protective clothing. Mansfield's last working quarry was on Nottingham Road, and it did not close until 1995. In production by 1832, it was owned by three generations of the Lindley family. Thenceforward it was known as Gregory's Quarry, a name it bore until its end. The photographs opposite were taken in its latter days: they are dated 1986, and although they illustrate a greater degree of mechanisation than the earlier picture they hardly show much modernity in the machinery.

Limmers farmhouse on Berry Hill Road was one of several such properties on the once extensive Berry Hill Hall estate. An 18th-century building, with barns, other outbuildings and a pond, it kept the name of one of the early tenants long after he died. In the left background of this 1890s view are two windmills on the rock at the top of Ratcliffe Gate. The farmhouse stood until it was pulled down in the 1960s and new houses were put up on the site.

Mr Sperry, who lived in the old farmhouse, is here harvesting corn in 1944, on land which would later be quarried away for the valuable moulding sand which lay beneath the Berry Hill area This photograph was taken from the back garden of No. 65 Berry Hill Road. In the left background part of Windsor Road and Windsor Cottages can be seen, and to the right a clump of woodland, which has escaped destruction in recent years when the end of quarrying has opened up the land for housing development.

The photograph above is taken from a similar vantage point to the photo of Mr Sperry harvesting corn, but 40 years later, showing the effects of the quarrying by the Mansfield Standard Sand Company Ltd.

Another view of the quarry which has now been turned into a housing estate.

A photograph taken in 1969 by Mr Purdy showing the very handsome building of Boots' main shop on Leeming Street. A dispensing chemist as well as a general chemist shop, it also had a library on the second floor for a while. Jesse Boot was a Nottinghamshire philanthropist who had successfully developed shops in Nottingham and then branched out into the county. At one time Mansfield had two other Boots shops in town: one on the corner of Westgate and St John's Street and one in the Market Place, as well as the main shop in Leeming Street. Now this site in Leeming Street is vacant, though there is a Boots in the Four Seasons shopping centre and one on the St Peter's retail park.

A view looking down Leeming Street in the 1930s, with the Horse & Jockey on the left.

The mediaeval cruck-frame timber building on the left of the photograph below was a blacksmiths in the 1880s and Caunt's Café in the early 20th century, while in the 1930s it was Ye Olde Refreshment House. Prior to its demolition in 1973 to make way for the Four Seasons shopping development, it was Bayliss's newsagents shop (pictured overleaf). The original curved oak support beams were unfortunately burnt by the demolition team. The King's Head Inn (also pictured overleaf) was listed in a 1793 directory and in the early 19th century served as a stagecoach terminus for a service to Matlock. It was bought by Mansfield Brewery in 1888 for £1,600. It too was demolished during the Four Seasons development, but a new King's Head was opened on the site in 1975, only to be closed in 1995.

Blythe's pork butcher's shop stood on Westgate and was one of several businesses forced to move when Regent Street was made in the early 1930s. This elaborate display at Christmas in 1910 was typical of such retail outlets, involving great efforts by assistants to position all the joints for sale on hooks. No doubt an eye had to be kept on dogs wandering free, and the police discouraged such arrangements on the grounds of easy pickings for thieves.

Mansfield Brewery, Littleworth

Mansfield Brewery was opened in 1855 in Littleworth on the River Maun. Water for the brewing process came from deep natural wells on the site. The company grew and developed a wide base in the East Midlands, owning more than 5,600 public houses by 1994. Unfortunately the company was taken over and closed in 2001, and the central building now houses a museum called 'Making It'.

Messrs Sansom Bros. & Co. Union Foundry, Union Street
The foundry was started in 1862 by the three Sansom brothers. The name changed to Stokes Castings in 1917. When the Four Seasons shopping centre swallowed up the works in 1973 they moved to Hermitage Lane but ceased trading as a foundry in 1977.

Sherwood Foundry, Nottingham Road
Sherwood Foundry was the oldest foundry in the town, dating back to 1788. James Maude, after whom the firm was later named, came to the foundry in 1840.

TRANSPORT

The motor car industry did not 'catch on' in Mansfield, though in 1909 there was a Motor Body Co., as this interior photograph from Linneys 1910 Almanack shows. As can be seen, the bodies were made of wood by skilled carpenters. Judging from the photograph, business was good, though working conditions appear cramped.

Berry Hill Lane marked the southern boundary of the town when this photograph was taken in 1961. The lane retained a rural charm with grass edging and fields not yet quarried away by the Mansfield Sand Co. The horse-drawn caravan was parked on what would become Chatsworth Drive, and it was recorded that the family asked for water from houses on Lichfield Lane when frost rendered their watercarrier useless. This is now one of the most crowded roads in the town.

Hermitage Mill Viaduct

It is not known who took these photographs in 1899, but they show the viaduct near the Hermitage Mill that replaced the old Kings Mill viaduct of the Mansfield to Pinxton line of 1819, which had too tight a curve for steam locomotives. The original timber-built construction was replaced by a stone one in 1899. As can be seen here, divers were used during this work.

he Diver

Hermitage

In 1910 the Bolsover Colliery Co., with the support of Mansfield Brewery, formed the Mansfield Railway Company to link the network of Bolsover Colliery mines from Kirkby to Clipstone. When completed, the line was run by the Great Central Railway. This was done partly to break the local monopoly of the Midland Railway and thus to ensure a fair price for the carriage of coal. The construction took from 1911 to 1916 to complete and, although built primarily for the mineral trade, it was recognised that there was a demand for passenger traffic as well, so an imposing railway station was built on Great Central Road, which opened in 1917. Although initially popular, especially with excursions to Skegness, the line gradually fell into disuse, and the last passenger train ran in 1956, with the mineral traffic ceasing a few years later. Virtually all traces of the stations, tracks and bridges along the route have now disappeared.

The viaduct, striding across the town centre and lit up at night, is a spectacular sight. When the Midland Railway built its station in 1849 they planned to lay a line to Worksop, though the route was not finalised until several years later. In the end, a 15-arch viaduct was built across the centre of the town, using stone from the Langwith cutting. The first train crossed the viaduct at 7.10am on 1 July 1875. The top picture was taken within a year or two of the opening, from where Dame Flogan Street now joins Midworth Street. It shows a derelict White Hart Croft and many of the equally derelict buildings that line what became White Hart Street. The lower picture shows the viaduct from the station steps. Even when there was no railway connecting Mansfield to the rest of the country, the viaduct remained a tribute to Victorian Engineering.

Buxton's photograph taken between the years 1890 and 1900 shows Mansfield Station, built in 1849 by the Midland Railway. In that year it was the terminus for the Nottingham line, but by 1875 the line was a tiny hub for the surrounding small towns and villages. In the 1960s, however, the 'Beeching cuts' resulted in a lot of branch line closures across the country and 10 October 1964 saw the end of passenger traffic on the line. The station was converted into Brunel's, a bar and Mansfield had the dubious distinction of being the largest town in the country not to have a railway station. Between 1993 and 1998, however, the Robin Hood Line was built in stages to reconnect Nottingham to Worksop. Mansfield's Grade II listed station building was bought back from the owners of Brunel's, completely refurbished at a cost of £900,000 and opened in 2001, winning the Railway Heritage Trust and Civic Trust Awards for Mansfield District Council in 2002.

The Pioneer was a brave excursion into the new field of Public Transport in Mansfield. That it failed is no disgrace. It was a steam omnibus that originated in Cowes, made for £600 by the Liquid Fuel Engineering Co., and came to Mansfield in 1898 on 30 June for the Mansfield Motor Car Co. Ltd, with the working service starting on 1 July 1898. The cost was roughly 1d a mile. It was commissioned by several prominent businessmen of Mansfield in the hope that, by making access easy to the town from the surrounding villages and towns, business in Mansfield would be promoted. Some of the businessmen concerned were W.J. Chadburn of Mansfield Brewery, F. Robinson of the iron founders Sanderson and Robinson and Charles Manners from Barringer, Wallis and Manners, tin box makers. The routes were between Mansfield and Warsop, Mansfield Woodhouse, Sutton and Hucknall Huthwaite. The bus could carry 22 passengers with another 22 in a detachable trailing car. The only problem was the solid rubber wheels. These did not last long and kept coming off, even after leather straps had been fitted which made the whole outfit vibrate badly. This insoluble problem caused the Pioneer to be withdrawn from service after two months of sporadic service. The photographs show a general view of the Pioneer, a close-up view and a sad, derelict chassis in the yard of Sanderson & Robinson, Leeming Street.

A much more successful venture into public transport by Mansfield was the Mansfield and District Light Railway Company – the trams! The preparation of laying tramlines and electricity began two years before the first tram ran. By 1905, on 11 July at 5pm the mayor, Councillor G.H. Hibbert, was at the controls of No.4 tram on its inaugural run to Pleasley, finishing at the terminus at the Plough Inn after an 11-minute ride. The trams eventually had five main routes, all running from the Market Place, and the frequency of service and cheap fares meant that the service was well used. The routes were Pleasley, High Oakham, Mansfield Woodhouse, Huthwaite via Sutton and Crown Farm (from 1911). In its heyday 30 trams were in operation, using as their depot the site of the now Stagecoach bus depot on Sutton Road. Some of the trams were single deckers; others were open-top doubles, while still others were doubles with enclosed tops. In bad weather the open tops must have been greeted with dismay, and it is on record that in very bad weather the drivers, exposed to the elements, suffered. They often worked a 70-hour week for approximately £3. The week-long strike in 1906 was peaceful and, due to the negotiations of the Mayor Alderman W. Singleton, successfully ended. There were occasional accidents – notably Skerry Hill, where the miners had to jump for their lives as the tram, gathering speed, reversed down the steep hill. The trams ran until 1932 when they were replaced by motor buses.

LEEMING STREET, MANSFIELD.

The old toll house on Southwell Road East, known in Rainworth as the Inkpot, was once a station on the Leadenhan, Newark, Southwell, Mansfield Turnpike Trust. Made redundant in 1867 when the route closed, it was in use as a dwelling until pulled down in 1955. Accommodation was limited, with two rooms and two cellars built with Mansfield stone. The walls were 20 inches thick. An adjacent Machine House was demolished soon after 1867.

Welfare

Following the Poor Law Amendment Act of 1834 the Union Workhouse was built at 105 Stockwell Gate and completed in November 1837 to provide relief for the poor and long-term needy, replacing the previous system of outdoor relief. Such institutions, in Mansfield and elsewhere, were widely regarded with fear and loathing by the public because of their meagre provision and harsh regime, although the staff pictured here in about 1909 look benign enough. The group includes the chairman of the Board of Guardians, Mr S.W. Skelton, seated centre, the master, Mr J.G. Hammond, seated far left, and the matron, Mrs Annie Hammond, seated far right. The last meeting of the Board of Guardians took place on 27 March 1930.

Union Workhouse, Stockwell Gate, later the Victoria Hospital, was demolished and replaced by the Mansfield Community Hospital.

Before the Union Workhouse came into use on Stockwell Gate, this undistinguished house in Meadow Square, on the west side of Nottingham Road, did service as a workhouse providing food and shelter for a very small number of the destitute who had nowhere else to go. By the time the Poor Law Amendment Act of 1834 came into force, which virtually eliminated outdoor relief for the needy, and with an ever increasing local population, it was clear that these premises were no longer large enough to serve the purpose, and they were closed in 1837 to be superseded by the new building.

MEADOW SQUARE

Elizabeth Heath's Almshouses

Elizabeth Heath, a widow who died in 1623, created a charity, which in 1691 provided for poor Quaker ladies. In 1844 six houses were built on Portland Street, and in 1855 six more on Nottingham Road, by Charles Windless. The first and second photographs are relatively modern ones, while that of the two ladies by the water pump was taken in 1900. The houses were modernised from time to time, extensively in 1960–61, and kept in good repair. As time progressed 'Poor Quaker Ladies' became hard to find so the charity was expanded to include any lady whose circumstances made it possible for her to apply for a house. The 12 ladies originally received 8 shillings (40p) each month, a new gown each year and a supply of coal. Elizabeth Heath's grave was in the rear garden of the Nottingham Road almshouses, as were some of the previous occupiers. All but Elizabeth's grave have been removed and that, most probably, is also gone now.

Hill House, on Commercial Gate, the headquarters of the Social Security Services in Mansfield, was first opened to the public on 13 November 1972.

Like most English villages and small towns before the 19th century, Mansfield disposed of its sewage by tipping it into the nearest convenient water-course, in this case the River Maun, but with a growing population and an increasing awareness of public health considerations this practice came to be seen as unacceptable. In 1897 an 'intercepting sewer' was constructed which discharged into the Duke of Portland's carrier. The corporation then built a screening chamber or 'settling tanks' near the outfall of the sewer, but before long this also proved to be an inadequate arrangement as the land became 'sewage-sick'. This picture records the beginning of the long-term solution of the problem: the start of the sewage treatment works on a site between Bath Lane and the Sheepwash, officially opened by the 6th Duke of Portland, from whom the land was purchased for £5,500 in May 1912. The duke is shown to one side of the Mace Bearer and the mayor (Cllr T. Hall) on the other. The borough surveyor at this time was Mr T.P. Collinge, although the plans had been drawn up by his predecessor Mr F. Vallance. The scheme was designed to cater for a population of 40,000, but permitting extensions to 80 or 100,000.

The Sherwood Forest Sanatorium for the treatment of consumptive diseases was built on Ratcher Hill, amid pine forests, ling and bracken, at a cost of £5,030 on 50 acres of land generously donated by the Duke of Portland, who opened the new facility in June 1902. As an additional kindly act he gave a pony and trap to the sanatorium so that the patients could enjoy open-air rides. It was under his chairmanship of the Nottinghamshire Association for the Prevention of Consumption that the need for such a provision was recognised and the first steps taken towards making it in June 1899, when it was calculated that 10 per cent of deaths in the county were due to tuberculosis. Open-plan wards and an emphasis on fresh air were essential features of the medical care provided. The first physician to the sanatorium and the man who had done most to get it established was Dr W.B. Ransom who, sadly, fell victim to the disease he had done so much to combat and died at the age of 48 years. It was decided in 1909 to name it the Ransom Sanatorium in memory of him and his father, Dr W.H. Ransom. In due course, as the fear of TB began to subside, the sanatorium was converted into a psychiatric unit, before being forced to close due to mining subsidence. It has subsequently been developed as a business park. Members of staff and patients are posing here in March 1908 and overleaf in March 1907.

The Fire Station on Rosemary Street was built in 1939 and officially opened on 24 May by the Chairman of the Fire Service Commission, Sir Vivian L. Henderson. The old Fire Station on Toothill Lane was finally demolished in April 1970. The Rosemary Street Fire Station was itself demolished in 1996 and replaced by the current building (pictured opposite/below), which was officially opened by the Duchess of Gloucester on 28 July 1997.

The first purpose-built hospital to serve the Mansfield and Mansfield Woodhouse area was constructed in 1877 on land donated by the Duke of Portland. That building later became a public house, the Fourways Inn, situated at the junction of Butt Lane and Leeming Lane (A60). The unassuming building pictured here on The Lawn (later Union St) served from 1882 as a cottage hospital, offering a mere two beds. The need for this provision was overtaken by the building of the General Hospital on West Hill Drive in 1889 (lower picture).

The need for an extension of these facilities was recognised fairly soon and led to the Jubilee Extension, for which the foundation stone was laid on the 28 June 1897 by the President of the Hospital Board, Mr F.W. Webb, of Newstead Abbey. The new wing, to be named the Newstead Ward, conformed to the then modern standards of design and equipment and provided accommodation for an additional 10 beds.

The official opening ceremony of the Bruntsfield Home for the Elderly on Eakring Road. The home was paid for by the Brunts Charity of Mansfield and was opened on 26 September 1974 by German Abbott JP. It has since been closed, demolished and replaced by flats.

Mansfield Cemetery

Mansfield Cemetery opened in 1857 on a 10-acre plot of land off Nottingham Road. The cost of the cemetery and buildings was £3,500. A further 10 acres of land were added in 1898, to bring the total cost of land and buildings up to £7,250. The photograph below is of the mausoleum, designed by T.C. Hine of Nottingham, for Colonel Thomas Wildman of Newstead Abbey. Colonel Wildman bought Newstead Abbey from Lord Byron in 1817, and over the next decades employed Hine to improve the run-down building. Col. Wildman died in 1859 and was interred in a vault underneath the mausoleum. In 2007 the copper plates bearing the names of the Colonel and Lady Louisa Wildman were prised off and stolen. In the background of this photograph is the family grave of Sir Edward Walker of Berry Hill Hall.

In 1984, when this picture was taken, the miners' unions were in dispute with the government's policy of pit closures and they demonstrated their opposition by a series of confrontations with the police. Divisions within the industry between different unions tended to aggravate the situation and inflame feelings. Public disturbances in and around the Mansfield area resulted in a number of violent incidents involving members of rival unions and the police. Pit closures and other consequences have left enduring economic, political and social effects.

In the days before Mansfield had its own Court House and before the town hall was built with suitable accommodation for Court hearings, Petty Sessions in the 18th and early 19th centuries were held fortnightly in various places on market days, most often in a room overlooking the bowling green at the back of the Bowl-in-Hand inn, pictured here.

When the town hall was built in 1836 the opportunity was taken to provide a room for the magistrates' sittings, so that Petty Sessions need no longer be held, as they had been hitherto, wherever there was a room large enough and conveniently situated, which usually meant a local inn such as the Swan or the Bowl-in-Hand or even the home of a magistrate. Living accommodation was then provided at the town hall for a gaoler and cells for a small number of prisoners, the lock-up being situated at the back, between the town hall and the Market House.

Built in 1873, when it was described in the local press as 'the most handsome structure the town possesses,' the combined police station and Court House stood at the junction of Commercial Street and Station Street. A brick extension was added to the old stone building in 1954, providing a main entrance from Station Street. Its functions – detention and judicial process – were separated and taken over by the new Court House on Rosemary Street in 1996 and by the present police station on Great Central Road. What was left of the 1873 building was finally obliterated by the St Peter's retail park in the late 1990s, except for one side of the police station, which was preserved and rebuilt, a rather meaningless façade, at the junction of Station Street and Quaker Way.

The old police station closed its doors on 31 March 1999, and the new one opened its doors on 2 April, having carefully avoided April Fools' Day!

The first sitting in the new Magistrates' Court House on Rosemary Street was held on 18 March 1996, and the official opening ceremony was later performed by the Princess Royal.